NINE DAYS IN HELL

September 1944: A British Commando in Arnhem

By Jeff Wells

Edited by Steve Davidson

Cover Illustration by Dante DiPasquale

Jeff Wells

Printed in the United States of America

First Printing, September 17, 2019

ISBN 9781692319496

Front cover image by Dante DiPasquale

First Edition

Wells Publishing
jwells@wishforourheroes.org

www.walkamongheroes.org

Dedicated to the men and women who bravely step forward to serve our great nation.

I am honored to Walk Among Heroes.

'Many times I have seen troops who are driven to a fever pitch – troops who, for a brief interval of combat, are lifted out of themselves – fanatics rendered crazy by rage and the lust for killing – men who forget temporarily the meaning of fear. It is then that the great military feats of history occur which are commemorated so gloriously in our textbooks. It is an awe-inspiring sight, but not a pretty one.'

-STAFF SERGEANT CLARK FULLER, SEPTEMBER 1944

CONTENTS

PREFACE

Fourteen years ago, I stood amongst a pile of rubble and dirt, observing the sights and sounds of Baghdad, Iraq. We, the soldiers of the United States Army, found ourselves stuck in the middle of a brutal war fueled by greed, religion, and competing ideologies. It was very confusing. Why were we there? What was our true mission? Who were our friends? Who were our enemies? During 2004-2005, the Al Qaeda-led insurgency was brutal, and as a nation, we lost brave soldiers, America's finest men and women, every single day. I had the honor of leading the incredible 3rd platoon, Bravo Company, 91st Engineer Battalion (Sabers), 1st Cavalry Division out of Fort Hood, Texas.

In my platoon alone, over the course of thousands of combat patrols, three of our brothers lost their lives, and more than a third of our platoon was injured so badly they had to be sent home to the U.S. for advanced medical care. Nearly every member of 3rd platoon was awarded a Purple Heart. Five soldiers were killed in our battalion, and many more due to suicide over the past fourteen years, as they struggle to deal with post-traumatic stress disorder and other aspects of mental fatigue resulting from a fifteen-month combat tour in Iraq. For the first thirteen years upon our return, I had no desire to talk about what we faced. I didn't reach out to any of our fellow soldiers, and I did my best to forget everything we had seen and experienced in that shithole.

Finally, eighteen months ago, we organized a reunion to bring our Saber family back together for the first time. It was a truly a humbling experience. As we exchanged stories, our experiences seem to have happened lifetimes ago, in a galaxy far far away. These experiences were very real, however, and many of our fellow soldiers are still scarred today, both physically and mentally, as they deal with those difficult memories.

As I began to accept my own past experiences in combat, I began taking a keener interest in military history, specifically the history of the other brave heroes who came before us. I visited battlefields, war museums, military cemeteries, read books, and began researching certain aspects of military history that interested me. I wasn't as interested in the politics or the wars themselves, but more the stories of the individual men and women, fighting on the ground and suffering through so much to accomplish impossible missions. I studied many dynamics of our nation's previous wars. I came to a very simple conclusion. As I write this, 6,951 U.S. service members have died in Iraq and Afghanistan. During previous wars, it was common to lose more soldiers than that in a day, or even a matter of hours. While each American life is valuable beyond words, for hundreds of years, American servicemen and women have blindly charged into walls of enemy fire, taken hills, and faced insurmountable odds in the name of one word: freedom. They have heroically sacrificed everything they know and love to ensure that we can live with greatest privilege in God's kingdom.

One particular period in history interests me above all others, the Second World War. Here, mankind witnessed the greatest armed conflict our world has ever seen, and God willing, will ever see. More than 300 million soldiers fought from more than forty countries across the world, resulting in more than fifty million deaths worldwide. To put this into perspective, the entire population of the United States in 1945 was 140 million people, which meant that across the world, the equivalent of one third of our nation was killed/exterminated. What was the reason for this staggering loss of life? A group of dictators used the atrocities of war to force their evil ideologies upon the rest of the world.

Their goal was not to persuade people to believe in their warped ideologies; people were not given a choice. For those who did not comply, death was the 'final solution.' Had it not been for the brave actions of a group of countries around the world, a coalition led by the United States and Great Britain, it is highly likely that we would all speak a different language today. It is highly likely that our society would not exist as we know it, and those of us born in the past seventy-five years would never know the incredible privilege of freedom. The millions of brave men and women who willingly placed their lives on the line have stories that are difficult to comprehend today. Having been in combat myself, I simply cannot wrap my mind around the circumstances these heroes faced every day.

Through my travels, I've had the opportunity to meet many of these great heroes. I've listened to their awe-inspiring stories, and I've had a difficult time processing them. I feel obligated to engage our youth whenever possible; to remind them of the sacrifices of these heroes who came before them. What I've observed has been incredibly disappointing. Our school curriculums barely mention World War II, if at all. The majority of Americans seem to be aware of only three significant events from World War II: Pearl Harbor, D-Day, and dropping of the atomic bombs. While these were all significant events, altering the course of the war, there were thousands of battles and millions of lives lost that set the conditions for these significant events to occur. In an age where our society tears down monuments, and attempts to erase history, I believe strongly that we MUST work together to ensure these stories live on. Without a basic understanding of these events, how can we ensure such atrocities will never happen again? Today, the youngest of our World War II veterans are in their nineties, and within the next decade, only a handful of these heroes will still walk amongst us. I made a decision to tell the stories of these amazing heroes. I want EVERY American to read these stories. I want every American to understand the sacrifices made by our grandparents and great grandparents. I want the younger generations of our great nation to read these stories and pass them on before they disappear forever. Most importantly, I want all of us to understand the circumstances surrounding these stories and the lessons learned, so that we can do our part to ensure nothing like this will ever happen again.

As we take a small peak into the lives of these 'giants-among-men,' there are many lessons to-be-learned. How did these men summon the inner-strength and fortitude to invade a foreign land guarded by the most powerful military in the world? In the midst of brutal combat, what were these men truly fighting for? In their darkest hour, what drove them forward? While most Veterans attribute their survival during the war to 'luck' or 'chance', I'm particularly interested in how they survived after the war. Once Germany and Japan surrendered, our men came home and attempted to piece their lives together as 'normal' citizens. During a time when post-traumatic stress disorder wasn't recognized as a condition, how did these men deal with their struggles?

These questions are particularly meaningful to me, as I've witnessed many modern-day military families torn apart due to the lingering effects of war. It's personal. In my unit alone, we faced brutal combat. Soldiers were killed and injured, which we anticipated prior to entering combat. We simply did not anticipate the staggering loss-of-life following combat. As I write this, soldiers from my battalion take their lives each year as they struggle to deal with the painful memories of combat. We have now lost more soldiers to suicide than combat, which is a tragic statement. Across our nation, twenty-two Veterans take their lives every day as they struggle to deal with life after the military. As we talk to our World War II heroes, how did these Veterans deal with these challenges? How did they cope and return to their 'normal' lives? How did they survive all of these years? During the twilight of their lives, as they look back, what lessons did they learn that can help our young men and women serving today? These are the underlying questions I will try to answer as I stand face-to-face with the greatest generation of heroes our world has ever seen.

Many of us idolize sports figures and celebrities as we watch them perform their God-given skills on television or the internet. We hound them for autographs and selfies, yet quietly living amongst us are some of the most amazing men and women to ever walk the face of this earth. We see them in passing at the grocery store. We stroll right past them in public parks and nursing homes. Men and women who, through their sacrifices, molded the world into what it is today, but are now mostly forgotten, especially as they grow older and have already lost many of their friends and loved ones. In our 'what have you done for me lately culture,' it's time we all come together to honor these incredible men and women, for none of us would be standing here without their sacrifice.

While I've had the opportunity to meet many heroes, and I have many stories to write, I chose to write my first story about the life of Rodney, better known as 'Rod'. You'll learn all about Rod in the following pages, but suffice it to say, Rod is an incredible man. Now an American citizen (dual citizen, actually), Rod grew up in Great Britain during an extremely difficult time, eventually joining the British Army at the age of seventeen. He fought alongside U.S. forces in one of the most difficult missions of World War II, Operation Market Garden. Made famous by the movie 'A Bridge Too Far,' this brutal nine-day mission forced Rod and his fellow soldiers into an impossible situation. They were literally left on an island to fend for themselves, with no support, boots-on-the-ground, and surrounded by the most powerful German tanks and weapons in existence at the time.

Today Rod is ninety-two years old, resides in Florida, and is one of the most cheerful 'ole Brits' you'll ever meet. We agreed to meet for an hour, then three hours later, we couldn't stop talking. Along with Rod's individual story, I referenced many excerpts from other books and documents detailing the circumstances Rod and his battalion faced during those ten impossible days. My observation when talking to these guys: true heroes like Rod often understate their accomplishments and are not comfortable bragging or boasting, which is why I wanted to include a third-party perspective of what Rod and his soldiers faced, provided by objective sources. My goal is to properly frame Rod's story to make the reader aware of all that was going on around him.

Please appreciate the story of this incredible hero. I've never met anyone quite like Rod, and I hope you will not only read his story, but also pass it on to those around you.

INTRODUCTION

As I sit in my friend Herman's living room in Florida, I anxiously await the arrival of Rodney and Maureen. 'Rod' lives next door, and his reputation proceeds him. He is known as one of the nicest men in the neighborhood, described by neighbors as a 'perfect neighbor' and a 'technical genius.' Neighbors tell me a story of this ninety-two year old man climbing on top of his RV to install a new roof. Other stories include motorcycle-racing, sailing more than 2,000 miles down the Eastern Seaboard, and his many professional accomplishments, including his role in developing prototypes of the Corvette, the legendary Avro Arrow fighter jets in Canada, and the first (and only) flying saucer. Who is this man? Possibly the most interesting man in the world.

Despite his incredible accomplishments, all of which I couldn't wait to hear, one two-year period of his life elevated Rod into 'hero' status, although he doesn't see it that way. From 1944-1946, Rod served as very young soldier in the British Army. Having grown up as a child in the 'Battle of Britain,' when Rod turned seventeen, he volunteered to enlist.

Finally, I hear a knock at the door. I expect a grizzled old war veteran to enter. Instead, a cheerful British man walks through the door, along with his lovely wife Maureen. This vibrant man embraces my hand and introduces himself as 'Rod.' I'm nearly speechless as I see this man who appears 20-25 years younger than his age. I hope to look half as good as Rod at half of his age!! Everyone walks to the back porch to talk. Rod and I take a seat on the couch. What follows is the story of this incredible gentleman.

FAMILY & CHILDHOOD

Rod was born January 1927, at a Naval Hospital in Gillingham in the County of Kent, Great Britain. His earliest years were spent in Southsea, Hampshire. When Rod was eight, his father (temporarily retired from the Navy) gained employment teaching celestial navigation at Calshot Castle, so their family moved to Fawley, Hampshire across the Solent from Southampton. Rod would ferry across the Solent to Southampton for work and after the war would live there.

Southampton, located approximately 111 kilometers (sixty-nine miles) southwest of London and twenty-four kilometers (fifteen miles) northwest of Portsmouth, is a major port and the closest city to the New Forest. The city's name is sometimes abbreviated to 'Soton.' A resident of Southampton is commonly referred to as a 'Sotonian'. Today, tourists flock to this city of 250,000, as Southampton is known for its massive boat show and the longest surviving stretch of Medieval wall. During World War II, Southampton was best known as one of the primary launch points for D-Day. Today it's known as one of the largest cruise ship terminals in the world. The city, highly coveted throughout history, has been occupied since the Stone Age and conquered many times over. Starting with the Roman invasion and conquering in 43 A.D., followed by Anglo Saxon settlements, and subsequent Viking and Norman conquests, Southampton has always been a popular place for 'foreigners' to visit. In July 1940, the German Luftwaffe added their names to the history books as thousands of bombers appeared on the horizon crossing the English Channel to bomb the British mainland in order to defeat their sworn enemy, Great Britain.

Rod was a young child during this very difficult time, living in a two-story brick home as part of a close-knit family of five. As the middle brother, he developed plenty of toughness competing with his siblings. Anthony, Rod's younger brother better known as 'Tony' (eight years younger, passed away June 2017 in Somerset, UK), was born in 1934. Kenneth, Rod's older brother known as 'Kenny' (three years older, passed November 7, 2006 in London). Anyone who has siblings knows how tough it can be growing up as the middle child.

Rod's mother, Amy Florence Johnstone (1900-1945), was a very loving mother who kept the family together while Rod's father was deployed serving Great Britain. Rod's father, Percy Simeon Thomas (1894-1963), has a very interesting story. Percy served two tours in the British Royal Navy. At the age of fourteen, he actually enlisted in the Navy with the rank of 'boy', which is an unusual concept in this day and age. Back then, the Royal Navy employed this system to recruit and develop young military service men. Percy served on submarines in both World War I and World War II. Percy left the Royal Navy and became an instructor, teaching celestial navigation as a civilian at Calshot Castle in Hampshire.

At the beginning of World War II, Percy was called back into the Navy, which led to many combat missions. In May 1940, as German armies advanced into France and subsequently pushed British forces back into the English Channel at Dunkirk, Rod's father sailed repeatedly, over-and-over-again, into heavy fire to rescue many British soldiers. In 1942, in Dieppe, he was listed as MIA (missing in action) and presumed dead when he was blown off the bridge of his ship.

Percy never wanted to talk about the war, however shortly after Dunkirk, Rod's mother received an invitation requesting his father's presence at Buckingham Palace. Rod remembers thinking about how great it would be to go to Buckingham Palace, but instead of choosing him, Rod's mother went to the West Country to pick-up Tony (he had been sent there for safety) and took him as her guest instead. 'I was so pissed!' he said half-jokingly. A few days later, the King of England awarded his father the Distinguished Service Cross, the third highest honor in the British Navy. The Distinguished Service Cross (DSC) is 'awarded in recognition of an act or acts of exemplary gallantry during active operations against the enemy at sea'.

During the war, Tony and many other children in Rod's area, were moved to Somerset, in the 'West Country,' for safety. Kenny enlisted in the Navy during World War II, and although Tony was too young to fight in the war, he joined the Navy years later. Kenny's tour in the Navy took him to the brutal Pacific Theatre. He was seriously wounded and walked with a limp for the rest of his life. Tony had a long, successful career in the Navy, retiring as a Chief Petty Officer, one of the highest ranking Petty Officers in the Royal Navy. Rod's father also retired from the Navy with a rank of Chief Petty Officer. Suffice it to say, Rod was the black sheep of his family, a lone Army soldier among a family of Navy men. Clearly, the 'heroism gene' was in Rod's DNA, however. This gene would rise to the surface as Rod entered his teenage years.

BATTLE OF BRITAIN

In 1939, Adolph Hitler, the Fuhrer, and his vast armies invaded Poland, setting into motion a black cloud of death and destruction that would continue to spread until the world ceased to exist as it was known at that time. That is, until a force of light was able to stand firm against these seemingly unstoppable dark armies, which later became known as the Axis Forces. Great Britain, a sworn ally of Poland, stepped forward to stand in the way of the Germans, and as a result, Britain paid a very dear price.

When the war started, Rod was a young twelve-year-old boy growing up as any normal child would during that time. His daily routine included going to school and helping his parents with chores. In 1940, as Rod turned fourteen, the German Luftwaffe (Air Force) began a massive bombing campaign against Great Britain and its citizens. Rod described the feeling as he looked over the horizon as a young boy and observed black specks in the sky resembling a swarm of locusts approaching the British mainland. As the specks grew closer, Rod realized they were not locusts, but instead German Luftwaffe bombers approaching Great Britain. 'We would see the bombers coming over in droves, then we'd see the Spitfires flying to meet the German bombers,' Rod explains. Rod then imitated the 'rat tat tat' sound of Spitfire machine gun fire, and explained that, 'planes were falling out of the sky all over the place. Debris fell from the sky and there were parachutes everywhere. This was a daily occurrence in Great Britain during that time. It was hell.'

Rod has many vivid memories from his childhood during those bombings. One Sunday, Rod left home with five of his buddies to head into downtown Southampton to watch a movie. Rod remembers the afternoon: 'I left home on a Sunday afternoon to go meet with the guys downtown, five of my buddies. At the time we all worked for British Power Boats [Rod worked there as part of a seven-year manufacturing internship program where he rotated through different manufacturing facilities]. We went to the ODEON Theatre. Halfway through the movie, they stopped the movie and made an announcement that we all had to find shelter as the German bombers were on their way. When we stepped outside, Christ, bombs were hitting everywhere. We decided to go to Johnny Peckham's house, which was located just past the Bargate [One of the original 'gates' into the city through the Medieval wall. Originally it was at water's edge. Today it is slightly inland.] about two miles away.

The center of Southampton was really being bombed heavily. The Germans were dropping incendiary bombs and parachute bombs, which were land mine-type things. When Southampton was bombed, the incendiaries caught fire, and you could see the city burning from France. So, once we decided we were going to Peckham's house, we held hands and just ran! Right before we turned the corner, we picked up this girl. She was terrified, like we were. I got ahold of her hand and asked her where she lived, and she lived in the same area. All of the sudden, we were about to turn, and.....[Rod makes a whistling noise]...down it came [a bomb]. Next thing I knew we were flat on our backs, and miraculously, none of us were hurt, just minor bruises. We got up, and I'm still holding on to the girl. I asked Johnny Peckham and Nick O'Connor if they were okay. Johnny said 'yeah', Nick said 'yeah, then I turned to the girl, and she had no clothes on! The bomb blew most of the clothes off of her. She was okay, just bruised a bit. I gave her my rain coat, she put it on, and ran off. I never saw her again after that, and I never got my raincoat back! [Rod laughs].'

When Rod was twelve, the owner of one of five houses in Rod's neighborhood decided that they needed to build an air raid shelter for their two families. Britain was short on raw materials at that time, so they decided to use the bricks from the well in their back yards to build the shelter. Rod was the smallest one, so they lowered him down into the well using a bucket, and he brought the bricks up one-by-one, which Mr. Wheeler (Rod's neighbor) used to construct an air-raid shelter for his neighborhood.

During another bombing, Rod's family home was damaged by a bomb that hit twenty meters behind his family's home. Rod explains that night: 'Our house was empty except for my mum and I. The Germans were dropping incendiaries all over the place. This big bomb came down right behind our house. I was in bed asleep when I heard mum call me downstairs. Well, she threw me under the stairs and jumped on top of me to protect me. When it went off, the entire house shook, we saw a huge bright flash of light, then nothing. We had a very large Chippendale mirror in the living room [Thomas Chippendale was a famous British furniture designer], and it was my mum's favorite mirror. When the bombing stopped, we made our way out of the house toward the shelter, walking over broken glass. I had never heard my mum swear in her life, she said 'The Bastards have broken my mirror!'. Her Chippendale mirror..that's all she was worried about! In the morning we came back in from the shelter and into the conservatory. There was her mirror, still sitting on the wall with not a mark on it! The back of our house was completely destroyed, but her beloved mirror was okay, and she was so happy!'

During that period of relentless bombings, when air raid sirens filled the air, and Southampton residents began to scatter, one story haunts Rod to this very day: 'I was fourteen years old and a butcher's boy delivering meat on my bicycle. I crossed this great big, flat heath [an open area of uncultivated land] to make a delivery. There were no trees at all, and I was completely exposed. All of the sudden I heard a roar, and right over me [as Rod motioned with his hands] about one hundred feet high, a German bomber flew by. The rear gunner was positioned at the back of the plane, and I could see him as easily as I can see you right now [he pointed toward me]. We made eye contact, and he lowered his gun and pointed it right at me. I thought he was going to pull the trigger and instead, he just waived at me and smiled.' Rod smiled and laughed. 'That guy was a good German. He had to be. I will never forget that moment, as long as I live.'

During that same bombing raid, another incident occurred that still bothers Rod deeply. One of the low-flying German bombers flew over the Fawley grade school, firing on the children playing in the schoolyard. Several of the little ones were killed, which saddened the entire town.

Also, as a fourteen-year old boy, Rod recalls being asked to help work on a nearby oil refinery. With all of the bombings, the oil refineries were easy targets, so the British government 'drafted' (for lack of a better word) men and boys, ages fourteen to forty, to help bury the oil tanks underground to protect them from the bombings and to preserve Britain's oil supply. The government pulled factory workers, welders, technicians and anyone they could find capable of manual labor. The tanks were in the process of being buried in the side of a hill as he heard the familiar sound of German fighter bombers approaching. Rod describes yet another bombing by the Luftwaffe: 'We were walking down the side of a hill, near the tent, and I heard the sound I knew very well by this point: A German fighter bomber. I looked up, and a plane flew right over and dropped three bombs. The bomber was so low, the tails of the bombs hit the ground first, then the fronts, and the bombs went barreling down the road, eventually hitting an empty oil tank. The tank was destroyed but it didn't cause any injuries. I could have touched the damn plane as if flew over. That's how low it was!'

During Rod's teenage years, there were massive labor shortages in Great Britain due to the sheer number of male bodies required to fight in the war. All teenagers were expected to work as a backfill for the severe lack of workers in factories across England to support the war effort. Rod was indentured to a company, 'British Power Boats,' and he assisted in the manufacturing of seventy-eight-foot torpedo boats and seventy-one-foot rescue boats. The seventy-eight-foot torpedo boat, better known as the 'Motor Torpedo Boat', PT-109, was the type of vessel Lieutenant John F. Kennedy commanded in the Pacific. On August 1, 1943, Kennedy's PT-109 was famously sunk by a Japanese destroyer, and Kennedy's heroic actions helped save many of his crew, ultimately propelling Kennedy to international fame.

MILITARY ENLISTMENT
& TRAINING

At the age of seventeen, against his mother's wishes, Rod volunteered to join the Army. His mother desperately pleaded with Rod not to join, as he was the only member of the family still at home. He turned seventeen on January 5th, and one month later, he walked down to the local Army recruiter's office to volunteer to join the British Army as a member of the Royal Berkshire Regiment. Several days later, they shipped him via train to Norwich for Basic Training. Today, as Rod watched Norwich play soccer on television, he said excitedly to Maureen, 'Wow! Norwich. That's where I did my Basic Training. That's where the whole thing began. It's a lovely little town.'

For the first three weeks in Basic Training, Rod learned basic infantry skills like patrolling and other Infantry tactics. One day, a non-commissioned officer (NCO) instructor pulled Rod to the side, handed him a 1917 Enfield rifle and asked, 'This is a 30-06 caliber, 1917 Enfield. Do you see that square post down there?' [the square post was approximately four inches in-size] Rod looked down range, located the target, and replied, 'yes.' Rod, having never fired a gun before, lightly gripped the rifle, pulled the stock into his shoulder, set his left knee on the ground, sighted in the two hundred-meter target, and squeezed the trigger. Rod and the NCO watched as his red tracer round hit the four-inch post. The NCO was very impressed and asked Rod how often he practiced shooting. Rod explained to the NCO that this was the first time he had ever fired a gun, and the NCO didn't seem to believe him. The NCO asked Rod if he thought he could do it again, and Rod replied, 'I don't know. I have no idea.' The NCO, assuming Rod's first shot had been lucky, asked Rod to fire a second shot. Rod sighted the target, squeezed the trigger, and bam, another direct hit. The NCO asked Rod to shoot one more time, and once again, dead center. At this point, the NCO was very impressed.

When the trainees returned to the barracks that evening, the NCO pulled Rod out of the building and took him to the British Commando [similar to our Special Forces] recruiting office not far away. The NCO, along with the Commando recruiter, asked Rod if he had ever fired a gun before. Rod once again replied, 'no,' and told the NCO's that his shots were just lucky. The NCO's had seen thousands of soldiers pass through training and it was very uncommon to see soldiers with Rod's skillset (combined with his physical fitness). They explained that Rod had a gift, and they asked him to join the British Commandos. In Rod's words, 'My face lit up! A Commando, at seventeen? You betcha!' Rod laughed, and next thing he knew, he was on his way to Scotland for Commando Training.

Having not even completed Basic Training, Rod arrived at Achnacarry in the Scottish Highlands and was immediately immersed into Commando training with a group of other young soldiers. The young Commandos conducted survival training in the mountains, learned how to conduct covert operations through mud tunnels, and practiced advanced navigation skills. Exercises were conducted using live ammunition and explosives to make training as realistic as possible. Physical fitness was a prerequisite, with cross country runs and boxing matches to improve fitness. Speed and endurance marches were conducted up and down the nearby mountain ranges and over assault courses that included a zip-line over Lock Arkaig, all while carrying arms and full equipment. Training continued by day and night with river crossings, mountain climbing, weapons training, unarmed combat, map reading, and small boat operations. Living conditions were primitive in the camp, with trainees housed either under canvas in tents or in Nissen huts. All trainees were responsible for cooking their own meals. Correct military protocols were enforced: officers were saluted and uniforms had to be clean, with brasses and boots shining on-parade.

After several weeks, the young commandos were transported to the Fens on the east coast of Britain where they were to learn and conduct amphibious operations using live ammunition. Rod's class consisted of sixty-to-seventy Commandos, several of which became his closest friends. The training NCO's separated the Commando's into small groups of eleven soldiers, provided a rubber dinghy for each group, and sent the young Commandos into the bay to conduct an amphibious mission. There were no motors on the dinghy's so the Commandos were forced to paddle to their objectives. Midway through the mission, the seas, very common in the English Channel, grew very rough. Rod remembers six-to-eight foot waves cresting over the side of his watercraft. One of waves struck the side of a dinghy occupied by Rod's battle buddies, and the dinghy capsized into the turbulent seas. Rod and the other Commando's struggled valiantly against the tumultuous waves to save the Commandos, but within seconds, the Commandos were gone. 'We lost them all. Eleven guys. The seas were so rough, we couldn't get to them,' Rod explained with a painful look on his face. Rod's dinghy was also floundering in the storm, but eventually it was located by a British Navy vessel, which towed the lost dinghy's back to shore. Rod and the other Commandos were in impeccable physical condition. In Commando school, Rod, with full combat gear and carrying a Bren, could run a mile in less than 6 minutes.

During that time, British Commando training lasted for five-to-six months, and Rod, thanks to his high level of physical fitness, handled the training with ease. In September 1944, several weeks before he was due to graduate, they sent fifty-to-sixty of the Commando trainees south to Dover Castle, along the southern coast of England. 'Dover Castle is a beautiful castle that sits high on the White Cliffs overlooking the English Channel,' Rod explained. When they arrived, the Commandos rappelled and zip lined from the tops of the cliffs down to a ledge approximately one-hundred feet above the shore.

Two days after their arrival at Dover Castle, Rod, Don, and George explored their new surroundings. They stumbled upon a banquet-type hall, part of the ancient castle. Walking into the hall, they discovered an old wooden door with an odd metal lock. Being curious young men, they pushed on the door, and to their surprise, it opened. 'Wow,' said Rod. 'I wonder where this leads?' Ahead of them lied a dark, winding ancient stone stairway. They left the door ajar to furnish some light and proceeded down the stairs. Finding another door at the bottom, they slowly pushed it open to discover an underground 'war room,' complete with maps, troop movements, and planners standing around the maps, hard at work. The three young commandos were immediately surrounded by guards and held at gun-point until their stories and identities could be confirmed. Years later in 1994, Rod and Maureen took a guided tour of the castle. Rod told this story to the tour guide, and after asking Rod a few questions to confirm his story, the tour guide's mouth dropped. He laughed and said, 'So, you're the ones! This door has been sealed since that encounter in 1944!'

The young Commando's conducted extensive hand-to-hand combat training, bayonet training, and other survival techniques. One day, the training NCO's transported the Commando's to an airport and explained that the trainees would learn how to conduct parachute jumps for their next segment of training. 'Boy, I hated this. I really did,' Rod said with a smile as he stared into the distance. The Commando's boarded DC-3's, which carried twenty eight paratroopers in the belly of the plane. Rod and his fellow

Commando's boarded the plane, hooked up their static lines and sat nervously awaiting the command to jump. Rod first jumped from an altitude of one thousand feet, typical for a combat jump. It was important to jump as low to the ground as possible to minimize time in the air and probability of taking enemy fire when jumping into combat. Rod was extremely nervous during his first jump, but once he exited the plane and the static line deployed his parachute, Rod breathed a sigh of relief and glided to the ground. Although he hit the ground hard, he thought to himself, 'wow, that was a lot of fun.' So, the next day, the Commando's jumped again, and then they jumped two more times in the following days, for a total of four practice jumps. After completion of their fourth training jump, the trainers gathered the trainees together and told the Commando's that their next jump would be for real. Having not even graduated Commando school, Rod and the Commandos didn't understand exactly what this meant.

'They gave us four jumps,' Rod repeated. 'Then after the fourth jump, it was real. Very real.'

The next morning, Rod and his fellow Commandos awakened and were transported by truck [an hour away] to one of the largest airfields in Britain at the time [Rod doesn't remember the exact name of the airfield, because there were so many temporary airfields built during WWII], where Rod saw more planes lined up than he had ever seen before. 'I'd never seen so many planes in my life,' Rod explained as his eyes grew wide. 'I asked the NCO where we were going, and he told me we were going to Arnhem. Operation Market Garden.' Rod paused for a second then repeated very slowly, 'Operation Market Garden.'

OPERATION MARKET GARDEN, THE PLAN

Operation Market Garden was the largest airborne mission in history, up to that point in World War II. British Field Marshall Sir Bernard Montgomery, the famous ego-centric British commander, planned the mission with the strategic goal of opening a clear line of advance into Germany to encircle the heart of German industry, the Ruhr area. More than 34,000 total Airborne soldiers would be dropped from the 101st and 82nd U.S. Airborne divisions, as well as the Polish Airborne Brigade, and Rod's unit, the British 1st Airborne Division. The objective of the airborne units was to capture and hold key bridges in the Netherlands to allow Allied ground forces to advance into Germany. The operation required seizure of bridges across the Meuse River, two arms of the Rhine, together with several crossings of smaller canals and tributaries. Rod's unit, the British 1st Airborne Division, would be given the most difficult task of all. Their mission was to capture the Arnhem Road Bridge, and to hold the city of Arnhem long enough for XXX Corps to establish a bridgehead across the Rhine. The Arnhem bridge was the lynchpin of the entire operation, which would allow free passage for Allied Forces into Germany. Rod's Division alone would drop 10,000 paratroopers that day, all destined for Arnhem.

To understand the full scope of Operation Market Garden, let's take a step back into the planning phase and political decisions made in the days leading up to such an aggressive mission. In late August 1944, Allied forces refit after their decisive victory in

Normandy, which led to a rapid advance into Belgium toward the German border. The Allies were attacking based on Eisenhower's 'Broad Front' strategy, which planned an aggressive Allied advance with two Army groups, Montgomery's 21st Army Group and General Omar N. Bradley's 12th Army Group. Montgomery advanced to the north, and Bradley to the south. Patton's famous 3rd Army was leading the advance for Bradley in the south, and he was moving rapidly. Patton longed to go through the German western defensive line, 'the Siegrfried Line, like shit through a goose' (Beevor 4).

Montgomery believed that all Allied armies should fall under his command for one massive attack to the north, but Eisenhower decided in favor of a two-headed strategy, which angered Montgomery. In late August, the only factor slowing the Allied advance was the difficultly in keeping Allied armies resupplied. Without proper supply ports established, the majority of allied supplies were being airlifted in, which meant the armies could only advance at the pace of the resupply missions. Montgomery, in favor of an airborne mission to spearhead the advance into Germany, had planned several missions, but they were cancelled in early September prior to planning Operation Market Garden. Bradley and Patton strongly opposed an airborne mission, because it would divert aircraft necessary to supply the stalled Allied ground advance. There was clear animosity by Montgomery toward Bradley, as Bradley had previously reported to him but now was his equal. On September 3, Bradley and Montgomery met to discuss future operations, and Montgomery agreed to cancel the airborne missions and promised 'all available aircraft should go to transport work so that we can maintain momentum of advance' (Beevor 7). Later that day, after Bradley's departure and contrary to their agreement, Montgomery instructed the 1st Allied Airborne Army in England to begin planning a mission, 'Operation Comet' to seize the Arnhem bridge, which would create a bridgehead over the Rhine River. Montgomery assumed that by being the first to form such a bridgehead, he would be given priority for supplies and augmented with additional American armies, making his army group the main effort of the Allied attack into Germany.

The First Allied Airborne Army had been assembled by the British and Americans on August 2, 1944, and Allied commanders were itching to deploy their shining, new, Airborne army, which consisted of six and a half airborne divisions, the most impressive Airborne force ever assembled. It consisted of the famous 101st and 82nd U.S. Airborne divisions, as well as British and Polish Airborne divisions. The Airborne soldiers themselves were eager to deploy, as many missions had been cancelled due to supply shortages, inclement weather, strategic changes, and many other reasons.

Operation Comet involved dropping two-to-three Airborne brigades nearly 110 km behind German lines to secure the Arnhem and Nijmegen bridges, while XXX Corps made their advance from Antwerp. Many British and Polish Airborne officers involved in the mission planning expressed deep concerns about the operation. Lieutenant Colonel John Frost, commander of the 2nd Parachute Battalion [consisting of 745 men, which Rod and his fellow Commando's would be part of], would ultimately command the troops at the Arnhem Bridge, and was completely frank with his commanding officers. 'Believe me, it will be a bloodbath,' he told them (Beevor 27).

On September 10th, 1944, General Dempsey, commander of Second Army, concluded that one Airborne division would not be sufficient to secure these bridges, and during a meeting with Montgomery, he recommended canceling Operation Comet. Montgomery agreed. He instructed Dempsey to begin planning a much larger operation utilizing the US 82nd and 101st Airborne divisions, for which he relished the idea of having both American divisions under his command. Dempsey immediately began planning 'Operation Market Garden,' which consisted of two separate parts. Antony Beevor, in his bestselling book, *The Battle of*

Arnhem: The Deadliest Airborne Operation of World War II, describes the overall mission for Operation Market Garden:

> *Market was the airborne operation, in which the American 101st and 82nd Airborne Divisions would seize river and canal crossings from Eindhoven to Nijmegen, with the big bridges over the Rivers Maas and Waal, the largest in Europe; while, further on, the British 1st Airborne Division and Polish brigade would drop near Arnhem to capture the great road bridge over the Neder Rijn. Operation Garden would consist principally of Horrock's XXX Corps led by tanks, charging north up a single road, with polderland flood plain on either side broken only by woods and plantations. They would keep going all the way over the bridges secured by the paratroopers. After crossing the bridge at Arnhem, they would occupy the Luftwaffe air base of Deelen. The 52nd (Airlanding) Division would be flown in, and from there XXX Corps would carry on all the way to the shore of the Ijsselmeer, a total distance of more than 150 km from the start line. The objective for the British Second Army was to cut off the German Fifteenth Army and the whole of the western Netherlands, outflank the Siegfried Line, be across the Rhine and in a position to encircle the Ruhr from the north, or even charge on towards Berlin. (29-30)*

That same day, Montgomery met Eisenhower, Supreme Commander of Allied Forces, at Brussels aerodrome for a meeting aboard Eisenhower's aircraft. Eisenhower's knee was injured, rendering him unable to exit the plane. Montgomery criticized Eisenhower openly for not slowing Patton's advance to the south. Montgomery demanded that his Army group receive the priority of supplies as the main effort of advance into Germany. While the two discussed these issues, Montgomery touched on his planned airborne operation, Operation Market Garden. 'Touched' is a generous word, as he only briefly described the plan to Eisenhower. They primarily discussed timing and the problem of supplies, which Beevor states Montgomery exaggerated to gain an advantage over Patton (31). In Eisenhower's usual fashion, he set the overall strategy and allowed Montgomery and Bradley to develop their specific missions within it. Eisenhower did not oppose Montgomery's airborne operation, but he also did not provide tacit approval, which Montgomery later claimed. Meanwhile, Dempsey finalized the plan back at British HQ and began briefing commanders to anticipate mission execution on September 16th.

History suggests that on September 10th, First Allied Airborne Army deputy commander Lieutenant General Frederick Browning made a statement to Montgomery that Arnhem might be going 'a bridge too far,' thus the name of the book and movie. Beevor states in his book that this suggestion is 'highly improbable, since they do not appear to have met that day. There is no mention in Dempsey's diary of Browning at the early morning meeting with Montgomery, and he had reached Dempsey's headquarters only at midday while Montgomery was with Eisenhower' (32).

Later that evening, Browning briefed the airborne division commanders on the plan, and made several key decisions. Most notably, he ordered commanders to prepare for the mission within seventy-two hours, a dangerously short period of time. Next, he made the decision to execute the mission in daylight versus darkness, despite intelligence that suggested 35% additional flack [anti-aircraft] batteries in the Market area. The commander of the First Allied Airborne Army, General Lewis Brereton had been excluded from the planning process, although he did attend the mission briefing. Beevor points out that 'astonishingly, neither Major General Urquhart of the 1st Airborne nor Major General Sosabowski had been invited' (32). To think the British airborne commanders designated to be the main effort of the operation were not invited to the planning meeting, is incredible.

While the largest Airborne operation in history was being thrown together in just a few hours' time, Rod and his fellow Commando trainees conducted their first Airborne jumps. Practice jumps described as 'fun' by Rod and his Commando buddies.

Additional questions were raised during the hastily-planned meeting. It was determined that due to the distance of the flight to the target area, each transport plane would only be able to tow one American glider, versus the usual two gliders. This very significant observation meant that it would take nearly three days to drop the full three divisions under perfect weather conditions [not common for Europe in September]. It also meant that the initial deployed Airborne force would be no greater than the force originally planned for Operation Comet, which was deemed too few troops to effectively hold these objectives more than one hundred kilometers behind German lines. This meant that German forces would have time to react and concentrate their combat power on the smaller-than-necessary Airborne forces.

The next morning, on September 11th, while Rod and his fellow Commando trainees were conducting their second practice airborne jump, in London, Browning briefed Major General Urquhart, commander of the British 1st Airborne Division. During this meeting, Beevor stated that as Browning finished drawing the circle around Arnhem, 'he fixed Urquhart with a deliberately unsettling stare, saying 'Arnhem Bridge – and hold it' (33). As Urquhart began formulating the specific plan for his division and analyzed the specific terrain around the bridge, he determined that it would be tactically necessary to hold the entire city of Arnhem, which Beevor points out, is much larger territory than usual division frontage (35), for a light airborne unit nonetheless. Beevor also recognized that 'Urquhart could not help wondering whether his 1st Airborne had been given the furthest and most dangerous objective as a compliment to its effectiveness or because Allied diplomacy could not survive a disaster to an American formation under British command. He strongly suspected the latter, and he was right' (35). Later in the day on September 11th, after Montgomery further complained to Eisenhower about a lack of supplies, Bedell Smith flew to visit Montgomery, where he gave in to Montgomery's demands and agreed to provide an extra five hundred tons of supplies each day, pulling from Bradley's and Patton's forces, which infuriated both American generals. Montgomery, having received what he wanted, informed Eisenhower that Operation Market had been set for September 17th, just six days later.

As the planning process continued, the drop zones were selected based on avoiding the strongest German anti-aircraft (flak) positions, which resulted in a drop zone ten to thirteen kilometers west of the British 1st Division's objective bridge in Arnhem. For light Airborne divisions, speed and surprise are their greatest assets. Landing, consolidating, then moving ten to thirteen kilometers to reach their objectives seemed to be a questionable plan from the outset, as it would provide the Germans valuable time to react and counterattack. It turns out that the Army Air Corps (the U.S. Air Force had not been created yet) dictated the drop zones instead of the units who would actually be operating on the ground. Very little consideration was given to the ground portion of the mission, which was the most critical and dangerous part for the Airborne soldiers. Meanwhile, Rod and his Commandos continued to train, having no idea that Operation Market Garden would be executed just days later.

All and all, Operation Market Garden was a poorly designed plan, from top to bottom. Montgomery involved himself very little in the overall plan and never took the time to examine previous failures from airborne operations conducted in North Africa, Sicily, or Normandy. In addition to the flaws mentioned above, perhaps the greatest flaw was the underappreciation of estimated German forces in the area. Montgomery's intelligence team underestimated the number and type of German forces in the area. Rod mentioned that 'our forces did not expect German tanks, nor were we prepared to face them.' In reality, Rod and his fellow soldiers faced many tanks. Even more costly, Allied leaders failed to account for the ability and desire of German forces to quickly provide reinforcements. While Allied Forces knew about the presence of II SS Panzer Corps in Arnhem while the mission was being planned, very little was mentioned during the mission briefing, as Allied commanders believed the Panzer Corps was mostly destroyed after Normandy. To make matters worse, Montgomery dismissed Bedell Smith's intelligence reports, preferring to use his own instead. German commanders understood with clarity, how strategically important is was for them to hold the Rhine. Allied commanders also neglected to think about what would happen if German forces blew the Nijmegen road bridge, a HUGE bridge over the River Waal. If it were blown, there would be no possible way for XXX Corps to reach Arnhem, and British paratroopers would be completely isolated. In reality, the Germans failed to blow the Nijmegen Bridge, a critical error for the Germans, and a complete stroke of luck for the Allies.

Unbeknownst to Allied planners, there were two weakened German Panzer divisions in the Arnhem area at the start of Operation Market Garden. Many of their tanks were not serviceable, and as Beevor points out, 'the vast majority of the tanks which Allied troops faced in Market Garden were not present at the start of the operation but were brought in from Germany with astonishing speed on Blitztransport trains' (Beevor 51)

German Field Marshal Walter Model, commander of German Army Group B, anticipated a pending offensive operation by Allied forces. Knowing the current state of his depleted forces after Normandy, on September 15th, he requested reinforcements to be transferred from the east to the west in order to bolster defensive forces in the Arnhem area. General Field Marshall Von Rundstedt, Hitler's Commander-in-Chief of the West, sent a message to General Oberst Jodl at Fuhrer Headquarters, 'The situation facing

Army Group B has further worsened in the last week. It is fighting on a front around 400 kilometers long with a battle strength of some twelve divisions and at the moment 84 serviceable tanks, assault guns and light tank destroyers against a fully mobile enemy with at least twenty divisions and approximately 1,700 serviceable tanks' (Beevor 63)

As the Germans began taking steps to reinforce their Army Group B, 'in England, the final touches were being put to the air plan which in two days' time would unleash the first lift of 1,500 transport aircraft and 500 gliders, to say nothing of the hundreds of bombers, fighter-bombers and fighters, whose mission was to destroy airfields, barracks and flak positions in advance. In the early hours of 17 September, 200 Lancasters from Bomber Command and 23 Mosquitoes would attack the German airfields at Leeuwarden, Steenwijk-Havelte, Hopsten, and Salzbergen, dropping 890 tons of bombs. Soon after dawn another eighty-five Lancasters and fifteen Mosquitoes, escorted by fifty-three Spitfires, would attack the coastal defense flak batteries of Walcheren with 535 tons of bombs. (As a comparison, the heaviest Luftwaffe raid on London during the Battle of Britain dropped only 350 tons.). Flying Fortresses of the U.S. Eighth Air Force would bomb Eindhoven airfield, while the main force, escorted by 161 P-51 Mustangs, would attack 117 flak positions along the troop carrier routes and the dropping and landing zones' (Beevor 63). Operation Market was a well-planned Airborne operation from the standpoint of air support and planning, but again, the shortfalls in planning would be exposed once the airborne troops hit the ground. Even in the air, in Rod's particular case.

On September 15th, according to General Browning's aide (and accounted by Beevor in his book), Captain Eddie Newbury, General Urquhart appeared in General Browning's office on the second floor at Moor Park and strode over to his desk. 'Sir,' he said, 'you've ordered me to plan this operation and I have done it, and now I wish to inform you that I think it is a suicide operation.' He apparently then turned and walked out of Browning's office (64).

On September 16th, Rod and his fellow commando trainees completed their fourth jump and were informed their next jump on the following day would a combat jump. A real combat jump. Meanwhile, Lieutenant General Brian Horrocks, commander of XXX Corps, gathered his commanders in a cinema across from the train station in the town of Leopoldsburg, to brief the plan for Operation Garden. Beevor lays it out nicely:

> This next operation,' he declared, 'will give you enough to bore your grandchildren for the rest of your lives.' The release of tension produced a roar of laughter. He then proceeded in the standard format to outline the current situation, enemy strength and own troops, before coming on to the object of Operation Garden. He described the 'airborne carpet' stretching ahead of XXX Corps from Eindhoven to Arnhem. The Guards Armored Division, supported by fourteen regiments of artillery and squadrons of rocket-firing Typhoons, would break the German lines to their north. Then they would follow the single road, what Horrocks called the 'Club Route,' which the Americans would soon dub 'Hell's Highway', over 103 kilometers to Arnhem. There were seven major water obstacles to cross, but the 43rd Division, right behind the Guards, would be equipped with boats and bridging equipment in case of German demolitions. There would be 20,000 vehicles on the road, and the strictest traffic controls would be enforced. The low polderland on either side of the banked-up road meant that only infantry could deploy out to the flanks because it was too soggy for heavy armored vehicles. After Arnhem, their ultimate objective was the Ijsselmeer (also known as Zuyder Zee), to cut off the remnants of the German Fifteenth Army to the west, and then attack the Ruhr and its industries to the east. As the ambitious scope of the operation became clear, reactions differed between those who were inspired

> *by its daring and those who feared the consequences of such rashness, advancing on a one-tank front (65-66).*

If Horrocks and his XXX Corps failed to advance in a timely manner, the airborne troops would be left hung to dry on an isolated 'island' with no support. Rod's unit, the 1st British Division would carry the most risk as they would be dropped furthest from XXX Corps. The aggressive plan for XXX Corps to travel 103 kilometers in just sixty hours to reach Arnhem, against heavy German resistance and possible demolished bridges, was extremely optimistic. Nearly every single variable outside of their control would have to work in their favor to achieve this timeline, something that rarely happens in combat. Rod and his fellow soldiers were told that Operation Market Garden would bring the war to a speedy end. Some officers even said they should be home by Christmas if all went well. 'Browning suggested at his final briefing at Moor Park that the strike north would cut off so many German troops that the shock would bring about a surrender within a matter of weeks' (Beevor 68).

While Horrocks prepared XXX Corps for the ground assault, Operation Garden, the Airborne commanders issued their final mission briefings to the Airborne soldiers for Operation Market. The Airborne soldiers were relieved to hear that the airborne drop would take place during the day. The Normandy veterans remembered the mass chaos that ensued as they were dropped and scattered miles away from their LZ's during the disastrous night drops prior to the Normandy invasion. 'A platoon commander in the 82nd Airborne described their briefing with the officers from Troop Carrier Command. Once Colonel Frank Krebs of the air force had finished speaking, Lieutenant Colonel Louis G. Mendez, a battalion commander of the 508th Parachute Infantry Regiment, stood up and looked around slowly. After a heavy silence he addressed the pilots: 'Gentlemen, my officers know this map by heart, and we are ready to go. When I brought my battalion to the briefing prior to Normandy I had the finest combat-ready force of its size that will ever be known. Gentlemen, by the time I had gathered them together in Normandy, half of them were gone.' Apparently tears were rolling down his cheeks by this point. 'I charge you all – put us down in Holland or put us down in Hell, but put us ALL down in one place or I will hound you to your graves.' He then turned around and walked out' (Beevor 68-69).

Lieutenant Colonel John Frost briefed his 2nd Battalion on a seven-meter model, constructed by Sergeant Robert Jones, detailing the Arnhem bridge and terrain in the surrounding area. Rod and other lower-ranking soldiers were given virtually no information on the overall plan. They were told to head to Arnhem to secure a bridge. The officers in Frost's battalion had many concerns, first being the location of the landing zone. Several of the officers volunteered to jump directly on to the objective, to preserve the element of surprise. The officers also knew better than to assume that the German resistance would be weak. Despite their doubts about the looming operation, Rod and his fellow soldiers remained in great humor, typical of paratroopers. Beevor mentions the old British airborne joke when drawing parachutes. The storeman tells the airborne soldier, 'Bring it back if it doesn't work and we'll exchange it' (Beevor 70).

Later that evening, Rod and his fellow Commando's knew something big was coming. They all had trouble sleeping. They tossed and turned throughout the night, not knowing exactly what to expect on the eve of Operation Market Garden. 'Paratroopers in the 82nd Airborne listened to a band playing, 'Some troopers were dancing on their own and others clapped their hands in time to the music,' Dwayne T. Burns recorded. 'Some were playing ball while others lay on their cots, dead to the world and oblivious to worry or to noise. It was going to be a day jump and we knew this had to be better than the night drop into Normandy.' The hardcore compulsive gamblers played on. Others sharpened their jump knives, made jokes about the Krauts suffering from lead poisoning or discussed their weapons, a passionate and deeply personal subject. Some paratroopers even had a pet name for their rifle or Thompson sub-machine gun.' Beevor continues, 'Lieutenant Ed Wierzbowski, a platoon commander in the 101st Airborne, had a troubling conversation that night. His sergeant approached him between the pyramidal tents in the marshalling area, where they had been locked down. 'Lieutenant, I've got a feeling I'm not coming back from this one,' Staff Sergeant John J. White said to him. Wierzbowski tried to snap him out of it with a joke, but to no avail. The sergeant was calm while his eyes revealed that he remained totally convinced of his fate. 'He then parted with a smile and said, 'See you in the morning, Lieutenant.'' Wierzbowski found it very hard to sleep. The look in White's eyes stayed with him' (73). Staff Sergeant White would make his final jump the next morning.

OPERATION MARKET GARDEN, DAY 1:

Airborne Invasion – Sunday, September 17, 1944

At first light on the morning of Sunday, September 17th, a massive air attack consisting of Mosquito fighter-bombers, Boston and Mitchell medium bombers, and B-17 Flying Fortresses took off to attack various targets in the Netherlands, including German barracks, airfields, flak positions, and troop positions. Rod and his fellow Commando's awakened and ate a leisurely breakfast of smoked haddock, a real treat for the British soldiers. After breakfast, the Commandos were transported to one of eight airfields utilized by the British 1st Airborne Division. Upon arrival, they were attached to Lieutenant Colonel John Frost's 2nd Battalion. Beevor explains that 'Frost himself had eggs and bacon. He was in a good mood. Having been dismayed by Operation Comet, he thought that this time the arrangements at least seemed much better. Frost, who led the highly successful Bruneval Raid in February 1942, seizing a German radar set in Northern France, had also known disasters in Tunisia and Sicily. He did not expect the coming battle to be easy, but he still ordered his batman Wicks to pack his dinner jacket, golf clubs, and shotgun ready to come over with the staff car later. He then checked his own equipment, including a forty-eight hour ration pack, his Colt .45 automatic and the hunting horn with which he rallied the battalion. Frost, a religious man of firm convictions, was admired by his men. 'There's old Johnny Frost,' they would say, 'a Bible in one hand and a .45 in the other' (Beevor 74-75)

Beevor explains that 'a total of 1,544 transport aircraft and 478 gliders stood ready for the first lift of more than 20,000 troops. The runways provided an impressive sight, with each tug aircraft and glider lined up perfectly for take-off. The troop carrier command C-47 Dakotas were also carefully aligned to become airborne at twenty-second intervals' (75). 'I'd never seen so many planes lined up in my life,' Rod said once again. As Rod and the Commandos lined up to board their C-47, they were given tea and sandwiches, which, unbeknownst to them, would be their last real meal for quite some time. Rod declined the tea for reasons he would explain later, but he willingly took the sandwich and boarded the plane with twenty seven of his fellow soldiers.

Rod described the sheer weight of the gear each paratrooper had to carry into battle. Beevor details the paratrooper's load: 'Paratroopers were so heavily loaded that they could hardly move and needed to be pushed or pulled up the steps into the aircraft. They had helmets covered with camouflage netting and strapped under the chin, webbing equipment, musette bags with personal items such as shaving kit and cigarettes, three days of K-rations, extra ammunition in beige cloth bandoliers, hand grenades and a Gammon grenade of plastic explosive for use against tanks, their own M-1 rifle or Thompson sub-machine gun, as well as mortar rounds, machine gun belts or anti-tank mine for general use, and of course every man carried his parachute behind' (76). Rod carried even more weight than the average paratrooper. Rod was a Bren gunner, which he credits for his survival during the horrific battle at Arnhem, but it also meant he was forced to carry three times more ammunition than the average soldier.

Finally, it was 'go time.' At approximately 0900 hours (9:00 AM), Rod and his fellow partially-trained Commando's ascended into the sky, having no idea what they were flying into. 'Three of us were in the plane together. George Joy, Don Spall, and I. Don was my best friend, and we all went to school together. I was sitting toward the back of the plane, on the pilot's side. We were all wearing Type X, Mk II parachutes. We approached the drop zone, and they told us to prepare to jump. There were twenty eight of us jumping, and I was on the opposite side of the plane from the door, so when they told us to go, I had to work my way around. I was probably number fifteen or sixteen out of the plane.' I asked Rod if they knew where they were going, and he replied, 'We only knew we were going to Arnhem.'

'Ahead of the paratroopers, there were 320 tug planes towing Horsa gliders carrying the 1st Airlanding Brigade, divisional head-quarters, and field ambulances, along with supplies and ammunition' (Beevor 76). A Horsa glider is a rickety plywood structure designed to tow behind a plane, then released for gliding into the landing zone. Gliders carried many men along with jeeps, heavy weapons, and other equipment. Beevor explains how the gliders took off, 'The tug plan advanced slowly until the tow rope tightened and then finally the glider began to move down the runway. The glider pilot would shout back over his shoulder, 'Hook your safety belts, the towline is fastened...they're taking up the slack...hold on!' Then with a lurch, a second lieutenant recounted, 'the tail comes up, the nose goes down, the plywood creaks, and we are barreling down the runway. Long before the tow plane leaves the ground the speed sends the flimsy glider skyward' (77). Can you imagine loading into a flimsy plywood box towed behind an airplane, prepared to take off into combat? Several of the gliders broke apart in the air, killing all of their passengers. Other gliders released at the wrong point and landed in England or the North Sea in-route to their objectives.

Rod was thankful that he jumped via parachute into Arnhem, versus a rickety glider. 'I sure am glad I didn't end up in a glider,' Rod said. 'They used to load all of the men in the front of the glider, and the heavy guns and vehicles in the back. The gliders flew in, and rarely did they land properly. I saw gliders break in half, tip over, and they were easy enemy targets. The worst part about the glider was when they landed and came to a sudden stop.

The heavy equipment in the back would come flying forward and would smash the people, killing them. It was horrible.'

Motion sickness was a huge problem as many of the paratroopers struggled to keep their haddock breakfast down. As the paratroopers looked down, they saw the coast line more than one thousand feet below, and they were suddenly over the North Sea. The reactions of the paratroopers varied. Some were very confident and boisterous, whereas others were quiet, trying to keep their nerves in-check. Many of the paratroopers slept, or at least closed their eyes.

My mind drifted back to my first jump at Airborne School in Fort Benning, Georgia [1999]. I remember boarding the plane, and everyone was extremely nervous. Before long, half of the soldiers were asleep! I never understood why, but I observed the same phenomena in combat as well. Many times, our soldiers would sleep while riding inside of Bradley's or M113's in route to an important objective. As soldiers, we mastered the art of sleeping in nearly any situation. There also seemed to be a strange sense of peace that accompanied a dangerous mission – a realization or acceptance that the coming mission could be our last. While disturbing for an outsider, as a soldier, it brought a sense of tranquility, and a satisfaction that we were giving everything we could possibly give. I believe that unrest for the average person often results from a feeling of falling short; a nagging feeling of disappointment that one is capable of giving more – of achieving greatness. I also learned early in my Army career, 'Eat when you have a chance to eat, and sleep when you have a chance to sleep, because you never know when the next chance will come.' The paratroopers preparing for Operation Market Garden had no idea how true this would be.

As the planes reached the Dutch coast, the flak batteries began firing at the approaching Allied aircraft, packed to the brim with paratroopers. The paratroopers observed the tracer anti-aircraft shells rising upward, almost like flying through a Fourth of July fireworks display. Beevor points out that 'the Netherlands was known as 'flak alley', because of the massive enemy anti-aircraft defenses guarding the shortest route for Allied bombers headed to Germany' (82). Many of the paratroopers were wounded by flack as it penetrated the exterior of their planes and gliders. If a paratrooper was wounded, he was pushed to the back of the plane to and returned to England for treatment, if he survived the long flight. The paratroopers and pilots were sitting ducks, hoping and praying their numbers wouldn't be called. The paratroopers' saviors were the Spitfires, Typhoons, and Thunderbolt P-47's who would nose-dive toward the flak batteries, guns and rockets blazing, attempting to knock out the batteries. The pilots displayed tremendous courage, often guiding damaged planes to the drop zones, while ultimately sacrificing themselves.

Rod and the British 1st Airborne soldiers flew along the Northern approach route, the fastest and most direct route to Arnhem [82nd and 101st Airborne Divisions flew along the southern approach routes]. 'The transparent insincerity of their smiles,' wrote Colonel Frost, 'and the furious last-minute pulling at their cigarettes reminded me that the flight and the prospect of jumping far behind enemy lines was no small test for anyone's nervous system' (Beevor 87).

At 1300 hours, the gliders began to land, released from their tow lines more than a kilometer from their objectives. The troops who successfully landed in the gliders secured the drop zones in preparation for the paratroopers' arrival. At approximately 1350 hours, Rod and the Commando's approached the drop zone and prepared to jump.

'We received 'ack ack' [a slang for 'flack' or anti-aircraft fire] as soon as we prepared to jump out of the plane,' Rod explained. 'When I jumped, my weapon was hanging down and I frantically tried to steer the damn thing [parachute]. We took sporadic anti-aircraft fire, flack, and I felt a pain in my stomach. I knew I was hit. I panicked. I thought I was going to die. I had never been in combat before, and I didn't know what to do. I learned later that they dropped us more than 8 miles from the bridge, which was our primary objective. I was hit right here in my stomach,' as Rod points right below his belly button. 'I was hit by a piece of shrapnel about the size of my finger-nail, and to this day, I have two belly buttons. Right here.' At this point he shows me the wound on his stomach, which serves as a permanent souvenir from Arnhem every time Rod looks in the mirror. 'I was panicked. We were only in the air for 90 seconds, but it seemed like an eternity. I thought I was going to die, and when we landed, I called for a medic. The medic looked at my wound and told me it was just a small hole in my stomach, so he put a patch on it and told me to get back to work. At that point, I thought, 'What the hell! I've been initiated already and we're not even in Arnhem yet,' Rod exclaimed with a smile on his face.

Suddenly, Rod's face grew serious and he explained, 'When we landed, I was injured and disoriented. My best friend, Don Spall, came running over to help me. As he bent over to help me, he was shot three times in the back. He fell over beside me, and I thought for sure he was dead. I said goodbye and we left him there thinking he wasn't going to make it. We had to move toward our objective as quickly as possible. I was very sad, because we had been school-boys together, and he was my best friend. I have thought about that moment for the rest of my life.'

As the spectacular number of planes, paratroopers, and gliders filled the sky, the Germans were caught off-guard. German reactions ranged from stunned admiration to fear and trepidation, as tens of thousands of paratroopers flew through the sky like swarms of locusts. Generalfeldmrschall Model was visiting German Army Group B headquarters at Hotel Tafelberg, when he first saw the paratroopers in the sky. Unbeknownst to the paratroopers, Model and his command staff narrowly escaped capture, as they gathered their belongings and bolted northeast in a convoy toward Arnhem. Panic struck many of the German soldiers, but

German commanders kept their wits about them and quickly mobilized forces to set up hasty defenses.

As Rod continued to tell his incredible story, my mind drifted back to 2004 in Iraq, which was the first time I (or my platoon) had been engaged in combat by enemy fighters. The first shot was extremely nerve-racking, scary, and very confusing. Nobody knew exactly what to do, and hundreds of thoughts flew through our heads. The second time we were attacked, we weren't quite as afraid, and we kept our wits about us. After the third engagement, the attacks seemed no different than any other routine task we grew accustomed to performing. Of course, it's easy for me to say now, but regardless, I can't imagine being wounded just minutes into my first combat mission like Rod. Being attacked is a very scary thing, and by the way, Rod was a seventeen-year-old kid.

Once Rod's 2nd Parachute Battalion had landed, within ten minutes' time, Lieutenant Colonel John Frost, commander of the battalion, summoned Rod and the soldiers of 2nd Battalion to his location. They gathered their forces and by 1500 [3:00 PM], they were moving through the Doorwerthse Woods in route to their primary objective, the steel road bridge over the Rhine River in Arnhem, gateway to Germany.

Rod continued, 'Lieutenant Colonel Frost was our battalion commander, and when we all landed, he gave us the order to move toward Arnhem. There was no resistance whatsoever on the ground. During our march toward Arnhem, people came out of their houses to greet us and cheer for us. The Dutch people handed us cookies, flowers and they shouted, 'I love you.' It took us six-to-seven hours to make the eight-mile march from the drop zone to our bridge objective in Arhem, mainly because the people kept stopping us. They kept hugging us, and I thought, 'wow, this is going to be a piece of cake!''

The Dutch people were so incredibly excited to see the British troops, and they did everything possible to help them. When the paratroopers landed, Dutch farmers helped free the tangled soldiers by cutting their rigging lines. They brought food and water out to the troops, as they moved toward Arnhem. 'Pretty Dutch girls kissed the soldiers, sweaty from the heat and the march. 'Everywhere the Churchill V-sign was used as a currency of friendship and greeting.' Cheering civilians, women and old men, offered fruit and drinks, including gin. Officers shouted orders that nobody was to drink alcohol or stop. Younger men emerged from hiding and begged to be allowed to accompany them and fight too' (Beevor 103).

As Rod moved along with the 2nd Parachute Battalion, Frost soon lost radio communications with his higher headquarters. The combination of trees and obstacles, along with German radio-jamming, made radio communication nearly impossible.

Along their initial movement to the bridge, as they entered Arnhem, Rod's battalion captured several German prisoners. Many of the paratroopers, including Rod, weren't even equipped with the normal Infantry steel helmet. 'When we jumped, they made us wear this leather thing over our heads. It was nuts,' Rod said. I laughed. I can't imagine going into combat with a leather hat protecting my head.

As Frost's battalion passed the rectory and church in Oosterbeek, C Company veered off to attempt to capture the Arnhem Railway bridge. As they moved to assault the bridge, a German soldier ran to the middle of the bridge and knelt down, apparently preparing to detonate the bridge. C Company charged the bridge, as they set foot on the northern portion, the middle of the span detonated and collapsed in their faces.

Rod and his fellow soldiers moved under the railway line from Nijmegen, and they began to encounter stiff resistance from Krafft's battalion in Arnhem, consisting of only 435 men, including officers, NCO's, and soldiers. 'By mid-afternoon, Model and his staff understood the full scope and intention of the Allied operation. XXX Corps had already begun their advance, so Model understood the Allies were attempting to secure a bridgehead over the Rhine. With that, he issued orders to secure the Arnhem bridge immediately. Model immediately requested reinforcements, which consisted of the 107th Panzer Brigade, and an assault gun brigade, rerouted while heading to Aarchen from Denmark. In addition, he requested a heavy Panzer battalion of Mark VI Royal Tiger tanks, 88mm flak battery and just about every unit available to be sent to prevent an Allied breakthrough' (Beevor 107).

While 2nd Battalion moved into Arnhem, the American 101st and 82nd Airborne Divisions were landing on their objectives. 101st Airborne would secure the first sector of 'Hell's Highway' north of Eindhoven in four locations near St. Oedenrode and Veghel. 82nd Airborne Division would be given the difficult task of securing Nijmegen and the Nijmegen bridge, allowing free movement for XXX Corps north into Arnhem. Once again, the Dutch assisted the paratroopers at every possible opportunity. Beevor tells the story of a young Dutch girl who assisted a gunner James Seabolt of the 101st Airborne. 'Dutch civilians ran up to help, and started to carry away a gunner called James Seabolt who had broken his leg in the crash. They and the Americans came under fire again. A few moments later, 'a beautiful Dutch girl arrived with a wheelbarrow.' Seabolt was placed in it and they trundled him off. He was in such pain that his comrades had to leave him in a barn in the care of the girl. They gave him a morphine shot and handed him a pistol, which seemed an unsafe combination, but they and Seabolt were all returned to American lines over the next week thanks to their helpers' (112).

Generalobesrt Student, German commander in the area, hastily assembled two battalions and sent one each to St. Oedenrode and Veghel to defend against the 101st airborne invasion. Meanwhile, 82nd Airborne Division, led by Brigadier General Jim Gavin, took heavy flak fire as they landed near Nijmegen. They encountered stiff resistance as they assembled on the ground and began moving toward their objective. At 2200 hrs [10:00 PM], 82nd Airborne soldiers entered Nijmegen and began encountering stronger resistance in the urban areas. Several paratroopers were wounded, and local Dutch citizens once again helped whenever possible, pulling the wounded soldiers into their homes.

Rod paused for a second to explain the overall mission, 'Operation Market Garden'. 'There were multiple bridges involved,' Rod explains. 'It was a huge operation. Many of the soldiers were loaded in gliders and towed. We jumped from C-47's, and I'm thankful I wasn't one of the soldiers loaded into a glider. More than 10,000 soldiers jumped into Arnhem as part of Operation Market Garden within a few hours of each other, and I believe it was one of the largest Airborne missions of all-time. French, Polish, British and American soldiers were all part of this mission.' Rod used a few props on the coffee table to explain the mission. 'There was a river with a main road alongside it. Across the river there were five bridges, with the furthest being Arnhem Bridge. The Americans' objective was Nijmegen Bridge, and they were very lucky. Two things brought the Americans luck. First, the bridge was rigged with explosives, and as the Americans began to advance across the bridge, the Germans pulled the plunger to detonate the explosives, and nothing happened. As a result, an entire battalion of Americans was able to cross the bridge. Unfortunately, they were still two bridges below us. On the Americans' other bridge, the battalion was massacred. The Americans used tiny boats to paddle across the river and the Germans inflicted tremendous casualties.' Rod pauses for a second and says again, 'They took tremendous casualties. They really did take tremendous casualties.'

Rod explained that he was a Bren gunner, the famous British light machine gun, known to be one of the most reliable and effective machine guns in history. Known as 'The Bren,' the British machine gun was a top-loaded weapon, sporting a bipod for increased accuracy with a range of 600 meters (and deadly accurate fire). With its signature curved magazines, the Bren (eventually converted to 7.62 caliber ammunition) was not officially retired from the British military until 2006. 'The Bren was a beautiful weapon. It was a lightweight machine gun that fired a .303 caliber round. You could insert a 30-round clip in the top,' as Rod motioned with his hand, 'or you could use a one hundred-round drum. The front had a tripod, and boy, you thought I was accurate before? You should have seen me shoot that gun. I carried two ammunition packages with 3 magazines in each pouch. Two more soldiers, the ammo carriers, also carried six magazines each. I had the option of selecting semi-automatic or full-automatic,' Rod explained, and his eyes sparkled with excitement.

Rod and lead elements of 2nd Battalion reached the Arnhem road bridge at 2000 hrs [8:00 PM], under the cover of darkness. Alpha Company, commanded by Major Digby Tatham-Warter, reached the bridge first and set up positions underneath the north end. He then deployed two platoons along the sides of the bridge to occupy houses and set security positions overlooking the bridge. Rod was part of a platoon that occupied a house overlooking the bridge. The paratroopers knocked on the doors and respectfully advised local residents to leave before the battled started. The residents were not happy when the soldiers began knocking out their windows, using furniture to create fighting positions, ripping down curtains and blinds, and filling bathtubs to ensure a supply of water, amongst other things' (Beevor 126). In-line with traditional Dutch hospitality, they still managed to the welcome the Allied soldiers.

Frost joined the paratroopers under the bridge as they secured the northern end under cover of darkness. The soldiers allowed German traffic to continue flowing over the bridge as they set their positions and were careful not to alert the Germans of their presence. The Germans were ill-prepared to secure the bridge upon 2nd Battalion's arrival. They only had a few men set up in the vicinity of the bridge, and despite Modl's orders, the Germans reacted slowly to bolster their security. Frost recognized a need to act quickly and decisively to secure the southern end of the bridge before the Germans could send reinforcements. The Arnhem rail bridge had already been blown, and the pontoon bridge south of their location had been disassembled, leaving Frost with two options: cross the river in boats or assault across the Arnhem Road bridge itself. 2nd Battalion was unable to locate any boats in the immediate vicinity, so Major Tatham-Warter deployed Lieutenant John Grayburn and his platoon to assault the main bridge directly. They stayed close to the sides of the bridge and attempted a frontal assault on the German positions. Rod watched in horror as a German armored car and 20 mm flak guns hammered the assaulting platoon, wounding many soldiers, causing them to withdraw back to the north end of the bridge. Lieutenant Grayburn later was awarded the Victoria Cross for his heroic attempt at securing the bridge. While Frost organized another attempt to secure the southern end of the bridge, paratroopers set up battalion headquarters and other fighting positions in and around the houses adjacent to the bridge.

Soon, a second attempt was made to secure the southern end of the bridge. This time, a platoon of combat engineers attempted to use a flamethrower to 'smoke out' the German fighting positions on the southern end. The soldier operating the flamethrower accidentally caught a box of ammunition (and possibly some fuel) on fire, which caused a massive explosion in the center of the bridge. The second attempt to occupy the southern end failed, but Frost was hopeful the fire had destroyed any explosives the Germans had planted on the bridge in preparation to detonate it.

Rod explained the paratroopers' actions when they arrived at the Arnhem bridge. 'We finally arrived at the bridge, and we were in for a big surprise. We dug in on the north side of the bridge, and we spotted the Germans lining up on the south side of the bridge. We did not expect tanks. We were told there would be no German Panzers in Arnhem. Our mission was supposed to be a cake walk. When we arrived at the bridge, we set positions under and around the north side of the bridge. We occupied as many houses as we could to provide security over the bridge.'

Frost's forces consisted of more than seven hundred men set in position around the bridge, but the Achilles heel for Rod's battalion, and also the 1st Airborne Division as-a-whole, was a lack of radio communication with other units. During the first night, forward artillery observers realized they had no radio communication with artillery batteries setting up to their rear. Knowing how critical artillery support would be, the paratroopers risked driving back through German lines to make contact with the artillery batteries to properly sight them along the German's most likely directions of attack. Beevor provides an account of a British gunner, who knocked on the door of a home and politely urged the residents not to be frightened when the guns began firing. 'When you hear a boom and a whistle it is ours,' he explained. 'When you hear a whistle and a bang it is one of theirs' (131).

The other battalions further behind Rod's battalion encountered strong resistance from the Germans as they attempted to move into West Arnhem. 'Model moved German reinforcements into Arnhem as quickly as possible, informing his commanders that the Heavy Panzer Battalion 503 with Mark VI Royal Tigers was being transported across Germany to reinforce Arnhem and Nijmegen. Another fourteen Tiger Mark VI tanks were also being railed in from Heavy Panzer Battalion 506 at Paderborn. Model explained the importance of securing the rail lines to allow for the reinforcements to arrive' (Beevor 133).

In addition to the Tiger tanks, Model and his staff ordered as many Infantry reinforcements as possible, redirecting several Infantry battalions, tank destroyers, anti-aircraft batteries, artillery batteries, and even flamethrowers, to Arnhem. Beevor explains the makeup of the German forces that Rod and his fellow paratroopers would soon be up-against: 'All through the night, Model's staff had been ordering in reinforcements towards Arnhem, using the town of Bocholt as railhead. The 280th Assault Gun Brigade, en route from Denmark to Aachen, was diverted to Arnhem. Other units included three battalions of around 600 men each; nine Alarmeinheiten of scratch units totaling 1,400 men; two panzer-jager companies of tank destroyers from Herford; six motorized Luftwaffe companies totaling 1,500 men; and a Flakkampfgruppe made up of ten batteries, with a total of thirty-six 88 mm guns and thirty-nine 20 mm guns. They were 'temporarily motorized' which meant that civilian tractors and tracks were used to tow them. The 20 mm light flak guns were sent forward to the landing zones to take on any more airborne lifts or drops. Model's plan was not just to block the rest of the 1st Airborne Division from reaching the Arnhem road bridge, it was to crush it between two forces' (133).

The Germans were aware that only a small force of 1st Airborne Division soldiers (Frost's 2nd Battalion) actually reached the bridge. The first priority for Harzer's Hohenstaufen was to concentrate all available forces on building two blocking lines to ensure that no additional 1st Airborne troops would be able to make it through to the Arnhem road bridge. While Harzer's forces focused on repelling British reinforcements to the west, Harmel's Frundsberg Division was ordered to destroy all resistance at the bridge as soon as possible. Harmel's mission was to deploy forces south across the bridge to reinforce Nijmegen.

OPERATION MARKET GARDEN, DAY 2:

Arnhem – Monday, September 18, 1944

A t 0900 hours [9:00 AM] on September 18, Rod and his fellow paratroopers received the German counterattack that LTC Frost had anticipated. Twenty German vehicles lined up on the south side of the bridge and attacked using speed and surprise. As they attacked north across the bridge, Rod fired his Bren machine gun at the approaching vehicles, in unison with every Sten and rifle available in 2nd Battalion. Beevor explains that 'The mortar platoon and the Vickers machine guns also opened up with devastating effect. The anti-tank gunners from the Light Regiment found their range, and the next seven vehicles were hit and set ablaze. Grabner's men, having never experienced a battle in such a confined space, tried to escape, but vehicles crashed into each other. A half-track backed into the one behind and they became locked. The open half-tracks proved to be death-traps. Their ambushers were able to fire down and lob grenades into both the driver and panzer-grenadier compartments. One tried to escape down the side bank of the ramp and smashed into a school building. Another crashed through a barrier and fell to the riverside road which ran under the bridge' (137).

The Germans continued their assault over the bridge with Infantry. Frost's battalion sliced and diced the attacking Infantrymen with their machine guns and mortars. After repelling the first attack with a decisive victory, a member of Rod's battalion shouted 'a defiant 'Whoa Mahomet!' This was the 1st Parachute Brigade's war cry from North Africa. 'Soon it was reverberating all around that bridge,' Mackay recorded. It would follow almost every engagement from then on, because it was also a good way of establishing which buildings defenders still held,' (138) Beevor explains in his book. On the second full day at Arnhem, Rod and his fellow soldiers displayed a 'swagger' unique to airborne forces. If the Germans planned to secure the north end of the Arnhem bridge, they were going to have to earn it. There would be no free gifts on this day.

The Germans did not wait long to attack for a second time. Frost's battalion was again prepared, although this time they sustained many more casualties than the first attack. From this point forward, Rod and his paratroopers would be under constant attack for the duration of their stay in Arnhem. Frost interrogated a German prisoner who told him that many more reinforcements were on the way. This was Frosts' first indication that his battalion must prepare for a nearly impossible battle.

Meanwhile, the entire city of Arnhem became a battleground as British forces fought valiantly against the more powerful German forces. The majority of the city was ablaze. According to Beevor, 'those in the northern part of Arnhem had no idea of what was happening in the center of town and towards the bridge' (139).

On September 18th, LTC Frost believed that XXX Corps would arrive in a matter of hours, and to accomplish their mission, they simply had to repel the German attacks for twenty-four, no more than forty-eight hours. Unbeknownst to Frost, XXX Corps would never arrive. Rod and his fellow soldiers were in for the fight-of-their-lives.

As Arnhem erupted in combat, Dutch civilians were stuck in the middle. Beevor explains how brutal the fighting was: 'There were many grisly sights. 'Smoke and fire darkened the streets. Broken glass, broken vehicles, and debris littered the road.' A para-trooper with the 1st Battalion described 'the smoldering body of a lieutenant' ahead of them. A tracer bullet had ignited the phosphorous bomb in one of his pouches and he had burned to death. A distraught father was seen pushing a handcart with the body of a child. 'A dead civilian in blue overalls lay in the gutter, the water [from a burst main] lapping gently around his body.' There were also bizarre moments in the middle of this battle. A Dutchman stepped out of his house and asked two British soldiers in English if they would like a cup of tea. A little further back along the route they had come, the bodies of British para-troopers lay 'everywhere, many of them behind trees or poles,' Albert Horstman of the Arnhem underground recorded. He then saw 'a man, about middle-aged, who wore a hat. This man went to every dead soldier, lifted his hat, and stood in silence for a few seconds. There was something terribly Chaplinesque about the scene,' Horstman concluded (140).

When the sun set on September 18th, Beevor explains how Frost motivated his paratroopers: 'Nightfall brought only a temporary relief to the British defenders. Colonel Frost went around visiting the different houses. He told the men that they could expect XXX Corps to arrive the next day. Some considered it 'our most enjoy-able battle,' as they recounted to each other how many Germans they had killed that day. But there was little opportunity for rest' (153). On day two in Arnhem, morale was high for the Brit-ish paratroopers. They had repelled multiple German attacks, successfully defending the north side of the bridge. Anticipating XXX Corp's arrival the following day, Frost believed the entire mission would be successful if they could hold the north end of the bridge for another twenty-four hours. Little did Frost know, XXX Corps was moving at a turtle-like, leisurely pace. As each day passed, XXX Corps would not arrive. Meanwhile, German reinforcements would continue to arrive, as the situation for Rod and his fellow soldiers worsened by-the-minute.

OPERATION MARKET GARDEN, DAY 3:

Arnhem – Tuesday, September 19, 1944

'For three days, we had a standoff between the north side and the south side of the bridge,' Rod explained. 'They attacked us continuously, and we would repelled each of their attacks. After the third day, the Germans conducted an all-out assault, sending waves of tanks over to our side. From that time on, all hell broke loose. Street Fighting.'

On Tuesday, September 19, a Parachute Regiment lieutenant identifiable only as 'David' wrote down some impressions while in-hiding after the battle. 'I was obsessed by recurring scenes of the nightmare passed – of Mervyn with his arm hanging off, of Pete lying in grotesque attitude, quite unrecognizable, of Angus lying in the dark clinging to the grass in his agony, of the private shouting vainly for a medical orderly – there were none left – of the man running gaily across an opening, the quick crack and his surprised look as he clutched the back of his neck, of his jumps so convulsive as more bullets hit him. How stupid all of this war game is, I only hope the sacrifice that was ours in those days will have achieved something – yet even at this moment I feel that it hasn't. It will remain a gesture' (Beevor 174).

David's quote was recorded as 1st and 3rd Battalions battled viciously to reach the Arnhem Bridge to provide support to Frost's 2nd Battalion. They attempted an attack through the night and slowly gained ground, but they were still unable to break-through. Both battalions were surrounded on three sides by the Germans and were nearly destroyed trying to reach Rod and his fellow soldiers. Meanwhile, the 11th Parachute Battalion attacked along the railway line, but they were also stopped cold by the Germans. The 2nd South Staffords [Battalion] attempted to support the attack, but also sustained heavy casualties. 'Soon after 1400, Cain [Major, Commander of the 2nd South Staffords] felt there was no alternative but to pull back. Not only was the attempt to get through to Frost's forces at the bridge defeated, but four battalions had been savaged in the attempt. With most officers killed or wounded, a chaotic retreat was under way. Men appeared out of the smoke of battle, running back in ones and twos 'like animals escaping from a forest fire' (Beevor 177)

Wounded soldiers from both sides continued to flood local hospitals as medical personnel couldn't keep up. As the wounded piled up, 1st Airborne Division still had no contact with the outside world. Frost's forces were pinned down in their fighting positions inside a series of buildings on the north side of the bridge. They struggled to repel the Germans, and they were sitting ducks, continuing to sustain heavy casualties. Still, they refused to retreat or surrender. The buildings were without running water, and medical supplies were gone. There were no bandages, morphine, or any other supplies. Battalion medical staff did everything possible to keep the wounded comfortable. 'One man just before dying of his wounds said, 'And to think I was worried my chute wouldn't open'' (Beevor 186).

A company of Frost's battalion was holed up in a school. 'Later that morning, the Germans bombarded the school with Panzerfausts. Thinking they had silenced the defenders, they surrounded the school. Mackay [company commander] told his men to prepare two grenades each, and on his command they dropped them from the upper windows. They grabbed their weapons and finished off any who had not been blasted by the grenades. 'It was all over in a matter of minutes leaving a carpet of field-grey around the house.' Mackay was recognized by his men as being one of those rare beings who were virtually fearless' (Beevor 187).

The Germans briefly ceased fire, and the German commander sent a captured British soldier to discuss surrender with Colonel Frost. In response, 'the English paratroopers suddenly let out a terrific yell: 'Whoa Mahomet!' (Beevor 188). They began firing fiercely at the Germans, more determined than ever. 'Frost was determined to fight on, yet because they were so short of ammunition he felt compelled to issue an order to shoot only when repelling German attacks. During the next onslaught a voice was heard to shout at the enemy, 'Stand still you sods, these bullets cost money!' (188).

The remnants of the four battalions west of the bridge were in full retreat as the Germans pursued with waves of reinforcements. Local civilians began to panic as the paratroopers dug slit trenches and set defensive positions around the Dutch homes, searching for any type of cover from the German onslaught. Back at the bridge, Rod and his fellow soldiers encountered the first two Tiger tanks advancing on their positions. 'The two serviceable tanks went into action that evening, guarded by panzergrenadiers from the SS Frundsberg. Their armor-piercing rounds went right through a house, leaving a hole in each side. 'They looked incredibly menacing and sinister in the half-light,' Colonel Frost recounted, 'like some prehistoric monster as their great guns swung from side to side breathing flame.' When the ammunition was switched to high explosive, their 88 mm guns began to smash the houses around the heads of the defenders. At times it was hard to breathe, so thick was the dust of pulverized masonry. The building which house battalion headquarters was hit' (Beevor 191).

By the end of day 3, XXX Corps had reached the edge of Nijmegen, which placed great pressure on German forces to open the Arnhem Bridge. The Germans had to take the bridge to move Panzers into the fight against XXX Corps. The Germans began utilizing flame throwers to burn houses and buildings in an attempt to smoke Frost's forces out. Still, the men held fast. The city center of Arnhem was completely ablaze. As the mounting German forces engaged Frost's battalion, they faced a firestorm of burning buildings around them. 'Chaos. It was hell,' Rod said. 'Pure hell.'

OPERATION MARKET GARDEN, DAY 4:

Arnhem – Wednesday, September 20, 1944

By day four, Nijmegen was ablaze, and Eindhoven was being blasted by relentless German bombing and artillery. On Wednesday, September 20th, paratroopers from the 82nd Airborne, in conjunction with XXX Corps, managed to finally secure the Nijmegen Bridge through a heroic assault across the Waal River, resulting in many casualties on both sides. Luckily for the Allies, the Germans had failed to blow the bridge, which ultimately allowed XXX Corps to secure it. Unfortunately for Rod and the British soldiers at Arnhem, XXX Corps would not push forward to Arnhem that night. 'Historians debate the reasons behind XXX Corps' decision not to advance to Arnhem. Regardless of the reasons, XXX Corps was too late in crossing the Nijmegen Bridge. Historians also debate the reasons behind the Germans failing to blow the Nijmegen Bridge. Some German officers claim that the plunger had been pushed, but nothing happened'(Beevor 220). Others claim that they left the bridge in-tact for tactical reasons. This strategic error by the Germans was the break that Allied forces needed. Unfortunately, XXX Corps failed to take full advantage of it.

Further south, the 101st Airborne also had its hands full as the 107th Panzer Brigade attacked Son in an attempt to cut off Hell's Highway. With supply lines severed, 101st soldiers were short on rations and ammunition. Colonel Hannah of the 101st

Airborne summed up the entire Operation Market Garden mission, as he 'was struck by the bad Allied intelligence, which had 'underestimated the enemy strength and degree of organization from the beginning of the operation. In every case, the Germans far exceeded the expected rate of reorganization, and were able to launch a coordinated attack with infantry and armor by D plus two [19 September] which was entirely unexpected' (Beevor 223).

As Rod and the paratroopers fought for their lives, there was no support in-sight. 'That night, Field Marshall Montgomery sent a characteristically confident signal to General Eisenhower: 'My appreciation of the situation in the MARKET area is that things are going to work out all right....The British Airborne Division at Arnhem has been having a bad time but their situation should be eased now that we can advance northwards from Nijmegen to their support. There is a sporting chance that we should capture the bridge at Arnhem which is at present held by the Germans and is intact' (Beevor 227). XXX Corps did not advance that night, and as a result of Montgomery's poor planning, the paratroopers were not given a 'sporting chance.'

Rod was nearly out of ammunition. The men had exhausted their supply of PIAT [anti-tank] rounds, their only effective weapon against armored vehicles. They had exhausted all food, medicine, and other supplies as well. The paratroopers, however, under Frost's leadership, believed that 'this is our bridge and you'll not set one foot on it' (Beevor 228). On September 20th, Frost made his first contact with division commander Urquhart. Urquhart told Frost that they were in a similar situation and could not reach his battalion. Urquhart had heard nothing from XXX Corps. Both men assumed XXX Corps would not arrive in-time. Frost began planning several options for withdrawing his forces, if necessary. Meanwhile, another German battalion of Royal Tigers [tanks] reached Arnhem, making life even more difficult for the paratroopers.

'In the school, Captain Eric Mackay issued two pills of Benzedrine to each of his Sappers but took none himself. 'The men were exhausted and filthy,' Mackay recorded. 'I was sick to my stomach every time I looked at them. Haggard and filthy with blood-shot red-rimmed eyes. Almost everyone had had some sort of dirty field dressing and blood was everywhere.' Their faces, with three days' growth of beard, were blackened from fighting fires. Parachute smocks and battledress trousers had been cut away by medics to tend to their wounds. Everyone suffered from terrible thirst. They had been drinking the rusty water from those radiators which had not been hit' (Beevor 229). Rod fashioned a dirty, bloody field dressing around his stomach, which he had been wearing for three days. Just four days ago, he was a young student in British Commando school training to become an elite soldier. Now he was pinned down without food, water, or ammunition, fighting for his life and the lives of his fellow soldiers. 'We didn't look forward to tomorrow or the next day,' Rod said. 'Our goal was to survive the next minute, the next ten minutes, and hopefully see the next hour.'

British soldiers were known to maintain a professional appearance, no matter how difficult the circumstances. They shaved and dressed their uniforms in the middle of battle. Very few British soldiers missed afternoon tea. Rod had long since forgotten shaving and tea. He did everything in his power to hold on to that bridge, to survive. The men of 2nd Battalion were on their own. They were completed isolated, and their only chance to survive rested on the shoulders of the men to the left and right. For Rod, that man was George Joy, Rod's friend and fellow Commando trainee. They talked, laughed, and suffered together, all of which kept both men going. The Germans described Rod's battalion by saying, 'Damn them, but they're stubborn!'. They also said their delay in eliminating Frost's battalion was due to their 'fanatical doggedness' (Beevor 228).

Later that day, Colonel Frost was in a meeting with Major Douglas Crawley when a mortar struck and seriously wounded both men. Frost refused to take morphine, as he refused to allow his judgement to be clouded. 'He ceded command to Major Freddie Gough, but all decisions continued to run through him. The pain eventually overtook Frost, and he was forced to accept morphine. The men carried Frost down to the cellar in a stretcher. Despite Frost's pleas to hold the bridge, the Germans finally took the houses closest to the bridge and soon were on the ramp. With no immediate resistance next to the bridge, the Germans began sending over the panzergrenadiers and Tiger tanks' (Beevor 230).

Beevor explains Frost's last actions as battalion commander of 2nd battalion, on the evening of September 20th:

When Frost awoke that evening it was dark. He heard 'some shell shock cases gibbering'. Many more started shaking uncontrollably every time there was an explosion. Apparently there was one soldier whose black hair went white in the course of less than a week from stress. The doctor, Captain Logan, warned that the building was on fire, so Frost sent for Gough and told him to take over command in-full. First, they would move those fit to fight and the walking wounded – only around a hundred remained – then Gough was to arrange a truce to hand the wounded over to the Germans. One paratrooper wrote, 'It was undoubtedly the right decision, but some men who were in a bad state felt aggrieved at being abandoned, even though the battalion doctor and medical orderlies were staying with them.

As soon as the truce began the Germans tightened the ring. They then insisted that they must take the British Jeeps to evacuate the wounded. By that stage Gough was in no position to refuse such a condition. When the truce to remove the wounded began in earnest, Lieutenant Colonel Frost re-

moved his badges of rank. Captain Logan went out with a Red Cross flag. There was a shot, and he yelled back, 'Cease fire! Only wounded in here.' The shooting died away. Outside, he explained to a German officer that they needed to get everyone out before the building burned down or collapsed. The officer agreed and gave his orders. As German soldiers came down the stairs, 'a badly wounded paratrooper brought out a Sten gun from under his equipment, complete with full magazine, with every intention of giving the Germans a fitting reception, but luckily he was overpowered and the gun taken from him.'

A German officer entered the cellar in greatcoat and steel helmet, carrying an MP-40 sub-machine gun. He looked around at the dreadful sight, and told the men following to help the wounded out. Both Germans and British carried them out before they could be burned to death. Frost was taken out on a stretcher and laid on the embankment next to the bridge. He found himself next to Crawley, with whom he had been wounded. 'Well,' he remarked, 'it looks as though we haven't got away with it this time.'

'No,' Crawley replied, 'but we've given them a damn good run for their money.' But Frost felt anguished at leaving his battalion in such a state. 'I had been with the 2nd Battalion for three years. I had commanded it in every battle it had fought and I felt grievous loss at leaving it now' (231).

During the truce, Rod and other surviving soldiers able to walk and continue to fight, withdrew from the brigade headquarters building to hide in the ruins of several nearby houses. Major Digby Tatham-Warter took command of the remnants of the battalion. Their new position was temporary, however, as the majority of the buildings were on fire. During the night, Rod and George Joy snuck through the German cordon in an attempt to reach the remainder of the division in Oosterbeek. Very few soldiers actually made it through. They were soon trapped in a small pocket west of the bridge. Rod paused for a second and stuttered as he tried to find the right words. He finally continued, 'We were in Arhem itself, and we were fighting from house-to-house. It's hard to talk about, it really is.' 'I understand,' I replied. Rod and his men held the Arnhem bridge for four days in an unwinnable battle. As they attempted to withdraw, the fight was just beginning.

In a sister platoon, Lieutenant Barnett had managed to escape the Germans by leading his platoon into a burning building. 'Trapped, they knew their only chance was to break out through the back, where Germans were waiting for them. 'I took a dozen or so [men],' Barnett recounted, 'and told them to fix their bayonets and we charged them. They were in a back garden and they got up and ran before we reached them. We were shouting 'Whoa Mahomet' and I think we scared more of them to death than we actually killed with bullets.' They made their way down towards the river to pass under the bridge, but suddenly they saw the unmistakable silhouette of a Tiger tank. They froze at the sight, and it took them a little time before they worked out that it had been knocked out and abandoned. They spent the rest of the night concealed under the bridge, as German patrols searched for survivors' (Beevor 261).

German 'Panzergrenadiers combed the battlefield. 'It was terrible,' wrote Horst Weber. 'The trenches were full of bodies. There were bodies everywhere.' Weber then discovered two British paratroopers playing dead. 'Going past two bodies I turned around to glance at them casually – and I met their eyes. I covered them with my pistol, and smiling I said to them 'Good morning, gentlemen. Shall I bring you your breakfast now?' (Beevor

261-262).

German soldiers continued to round up paratroopers. When taken prisoner, Jewish paratroopers either sported fake dog tags or traded their dog tags for those of a dead soldier. Despite the brutal fighting, there was a high level of respect between the paratroopers and the German attackers. At one POW collection point, 'Occasionally one [German soldier] would stop and pat a British soldier on the shoulder and offer his congratulations. 'Nice fight, Tommy,' a German officer said' (Beevor 262).

Rod explained that, 'After LTC Frost was captured, we moved west. George and I were totally on our own. We cleared one building after another, going house-to-house, in close quarter fighting. It was very confusing. I remember a German jumping out from behind a building right in front of me. I was face-to-face with him. I just reacted. I shot him with my Bren. I remember the top of his head blowing off against the wall and blood spattering everywhere.'

Rod recalled another story in Arnhem, which he began by saying, 'I was terrified!' He continued the story, 'We were street fighting in Arnhem, going from house-to-house. I was hiding behind this house. There was enemy fire all around, and all of the sudden, the house next to me began shaking. I wondered, 'what the hell is happening?' I turned to George Joy and asked him what was going on, and he responded with a shrug of his shoulders. All of the sudden, the whole house collapsed and this huge Royal Tiger tank came rumbling out. We were so scared, we took off running. I'm positive I ran a four-minute mile long before Roger Bannister ever did!' Rod laughed and continued, 'Thankfully the Tiger's turret was pointed the other direction, but George and I ran a mile in seconds!' Rod laughed again, and I responded by saying, 'Rod, you may have run the first and only three-minute mile in the history of the world!'

Rod discussed the difficulties involved in urban combat. I talked about the mass chaos we faced in Baghdad while fighting in urban terrain. Rod frankly stated, 'Well, at least we knew who we were fighting. We were fighting the Germans. You guys had no idea who was good or bad. You didn't know who the hell you were fighting.' While this may be partly true, I wouldn't love the idea of fighting an armored force, 10 times our size, in a heavily urban environment with no food, water, or ammunition.

As a Bren gunner, Rod was critical to the survival of his fellow soldiers. As an Airborne operation, the soldiers jumped into Arnhem with a limited quantity of ammunition. They relied upon resupply missions, usually dropped from the air. Rod's unit had established predesignated drop locations with the pilots, but once the mission began falling apart, communication was completely broken with the aircraft. The planes would inevitably drop the supplies in the wrong place, usually into German hands. 'It was horrible. It was so screwed up,' Rod said. 'If we had been able to get more supplies, we may have been able to hold the bridge. We ran out of food and ammunition, and we kept watching the planes fly over and drop supplies behind German lines. Our own planes dropped ALL of our food and ammunition right into their hands. The Germans loved it, and I think they ate like kings!' I asked Rod why the Allied planes kept dropping the supplies in the wrong place, and he remembered a story, 'We were set up in a tower next to the bridge. I remained in place, but the guys in the adjacent tower moved to a nearby park to mark a new drop zone for the supplies. They used smoke and other markings to signal the new drop location to the planes, but lo and behold, when the planes actually flew over, they ignored our markings and dropped the supplies in the location they were originally told to drop, which was right into the hands of the Germans. I don't know why, but we had zero radio communication with the planes. The radios just didn't work.'

Beevor explains the primary reason for the supply shortages: 'The key problem came from the supply containers dropping outside the perimeter, because the lack of radio contact meant that the RAF did not have a clear idea of the defended area. Smoke from the fighting obscured the colored panels, and it was no good firing Very Lights or setting off smoke grenades because the Germans were doing the same, having captured the plans which revealed all of the signals. And when containers were retrieved, they often lacked food. 'Resupply has come in,' wrote Corporal George Cosadinos, 'but the majority dropped in the wrong place. All we received were 6 pounder [anti-tank] shells. You can't eat them!' Even greater fury was provoked by containers, filled not with food or ammunition, but with maroon berets, battledress, belts, and even blanco' (269).

Despite the breakdown in communication, the heroism of the pilots dropping the supplies should not be understated. They frequently sacrificed their lives to resupply the paratroopers. 'Everyone's attention was on the sky when the RAF supply planes approached, and many admitted to having their heart in their mouth, imagining the bravery required to keep the plane on course through the fire from the surrounding flak batteries [now reinforced]. 'My eye caught one of the burning Dakotas,' wrote Lance Bombardier Jones. 'For the briefest second two figures appeared at the doorway. One had a chute and the other didn't and they were jumping on the one chute. As they came out of the doorway, they parted. The one floated down in his chute; the other fell to earth like a stone. I can still picture him falling, his arms akimbo, diving headfirst toward the ground' (Beevor 270).

Reeling from casualties sustained trying to reach Frost's battalion, the 4th Parachute Brigade, commanded by Colonel Hackett, continued to fight for its life south of the railway line. Beevor describes the humor displayed by these incredible Airborne soldiers, despite the impossible circumstances: 'Late in the afternoon, during a slight lull after another attack, the defenders were surprised to hear music through the trees. A German loudspeaker van was playing Glen Miller's 'In the Mood'. The paratroopers were even more amused when it was replaced by a voice calling to them in English. 'Gentlemen of the 1st Airborne Division, remember your wives and sweethearts at home.' It then tried to claim that many of their senior officers, including General Urquhart, had been captured, so it was perfectly honorable for them to surrender. This provoked catcalls and insults and whistling, then firing. 'Stayed in position all day,' wrote a paratrooper called Mollett. Plenty of mortaring and sniper fire, so made myself a humdinger of a little trench....Got another cert [confirmed kill] when a bunch of Jerries came right out into the open in front of us, also several possible. Heard a mobile speaker in the distance – funny shooting Jerries to dance music' (236).

After four days of brutal fighting against insurmountable odds, the mental burden carried by Rod and his fellow soldiers was unimaginable. 'Psychological breakdown from combat fatigue could produce many strange forms of behavior. One man, although hardly wounded physically, would take off all his clothes and walk around the room, pumping his arms and making noises like a locomotive. From time to time, he would utter a string of curses and say, 'Blast this fireman, he was never any good.' Another casualty would wake people at night, bend over them and stare into their eyes to ask, 'Have you got faith?' At the St. Elizabeth Hospital, Sister Stransky had a strange encounter with a case of German combat fatigue. A Wehrmacht soldier appeared armed with a pistol. Sister Stransky, a Viennese, refused to allow him to come in. He kept repeating to her, 'I have come all the way from Siberia with a new weapon to rescue the Fuhrer.' When still refused entry, he sat down on the steps of the hospital entrance and began sobbing. Some died with great calm. A sergeant who knew he was dying said to a medic, 'I know I'm not going to live. Would you please just hold my hand' (Beevor 243).

OPERATION MARKET GARDEN, DAY 5:

Arnhem – Thursday, September 21, 1944

On September 21st, an additional forty-five German Royal Tiger tanks moved into Arnhem, making the situation even more dangerous for Rod and the small pockets of paratroopers still evading captivity. Rod and George finally stumbled upon friendly forces near Oosterbeek. The fighting was vicious there as well, as intense urban combat became the order-of-the-day. 'The new positions turned into a suburban battlefield in which self-propelled assault guns would dominate the street, and house-to-house fighting became savagely intimate. British soldiers claimed that they could tell if Germans were present purely from the smell of stale tobacco' (Beevor 268).

'By dusk our sole remaining anti-tank gun was knocked out and a bloody Tiger was still whining around just over the crest. We waited for it with 82 grenades, but it did not come in, and glad we were when a Polish anti-tank gun and crew appeared and dug in among us. The remnants of 1st Airborne Division, as far as we can make out, are now holding a box some one and a half miles square, with Jerry on three sides and the Rhine on the fourth' (Beevor 276).

OPERATION MARKET GARDEN, DAY 6:

Arnhem – Friday, September 22, 1944

A fter not sleeping for five days, Rod and his fellow soldiers were mentally and physically exhausted. Covered in blood from head-to-toe, starving, and thirsty, they sipped on rusty water from radiators inside local Arnhem homes. Long since overrun, they were no longer focused on defeating the Germans in Arnhem. The paratroopers were focused on survival, the most basic of all instincts. Survival from one minute to the next. Rod's sole focus was to evade capture for as long as possible.

Friday, September 22nd, became known as 'Black Friday' as the Germans began three days of vicious attacks on the 82nd and 101st Airborne Divisions along 'Hell's Highway.' Meanwhile, in Oosterbeek, Major General Urquhart sent his chief of staff, Lieutenant Colonel Charles Mackenzie across the Neder Rijn. Mackenzie would move to Nijmegen to meet Browning and XXX Corps commander, Horrocks, in-person to describe 1st Airborne Division's desperate situation. The division had become a collection of random soldiers hanging on with no supplies or ammunition. XXX Corps was so close and yet so incredibly far away.

Rod, George and the small group of commandos continued to hang on, moving and fighting from house-to-house. Rod was working on his sixth day without sleep, barely able to stand and walk forward. Adrenaline alone kept him awake. Throughout our conversation, I never head Rod refer to himself as a 'hero' or 'brave.' Perhaps the most accurate description of Rod and his fellow soldiers came from a German major and veteran of World War I, as he addressed his fellow German soldiers and referred to the British 1st Airborne Division: 'These men have stood up under the most terrible artillery bombardment I have ever seen. They have fought on without food and without sleep for several days. Even though they are our enemies, they are the bravest men I have ever seen. When you complain, you make me feel ashamed of being German. I suggest that you be quiet and follow their example' (Beevor 284).

It's important to recognize the sacrifices made by Dutch citizens to assist Rod and his fellow soldiers in the heat of combat, as their homes burned to the ground. Many citizens could have evacuated before the heavy fighting began, but they chose to stay and help the Allies. Dutch underground resistance members helped to covertly retrieve supplies dropped behind German lines. They also assisted in providing the locations of German positions. Perhaps the greatest hero of Operation Market Garden was a Dutch civilian, Kate ter Horst. In her house, located next to Oosterbeek Church, she set up an aid station to treat wounded soldiers. 'The walls were pockmarked all over by rifle fire and they had fifty-seven fatal casualties piled in the garden, giving off the sickly-sweet smell of decaying corpses. This 'tall slim Dutchwoman with the blond hair and the calm ice-blue eyes' became known as the 'Angel of Arnhem.' She helped care for 250 men brought to the regimental aid post set up in her house, even though she had five children to look after. She comforted the wounded and dying by reading aloud from a Bible in the King James version. Her voice and the fine, familiar prose calmed the fears of all who listened to her' (Beevor 289).

Beevor tells a funny story that took place during a not-so-fun time, highlighting the friendliness of the Dutch people: 'Even in the midst of furious fighting, a Dutch family asked PFC John Cipolla to join them for dinner. He could not resist the invitation to a table laid with a tablecloth. Just after they had sat down, his Top Sergeant glanced in as he passed the window, carried on a couple paces, did a double-take and then dashed back to yell at him that he should get his butt outside where he belonged. Cipolla grabbed a chicken leg and his rifle, thanked the family, and ran for the door' (Beevor 279).

Also on September 22, just one day after sending a message to Eisenhower stating that the paratroopers still had a 'sporting chance' of taking the Arnhem Bridge, Montgomery wrote in his diary: 'I am very doubtful myself now if they [1st Airborne] will be able to hold out, and we may have to withdraw them' (Beevor 292). Through the entire battle, Montgomery never made an effort to visit Horrocks, or any other commander on the front lines, which historians believe was intended to distance himself from the tragedy unfolding in Arnhem.

OPERATION MARKET GARDEN, DAY 7:

Arnhem – Saturday, September 23, 1944

On September 23, the XXX Corps advance was completely halted by German attacks. XXX Corps was taking casualties at rates much faster than they could evacuate their wounded on 'Hell's Highway.' British Airborne casualties were unable to be evacuated from Oosterbeek, where medical supplies had been exhausted. Soldiers moaned in pain, with no morphine left to calm the wounded. Soldiers with severed limbs began suffering from gangrene, with no antibiotics to slow the flesh-eating disease.

Low on ammunition, Rod and George hunkered down in a house, doing their best to hide during the day. They conserved ammunition by only engaging German fighters within range of Rod's Bren. At this point, nothing surprised them. The sight of blood everywhere, combined with constant artillery and tank fire would rattle nearly anyone. Not Rod. He was desensitized to the sights and sounds of war, almost like a zombie. Just an innocent seventeen-year-old kid eight days before, Rod was now a battle-hardened warrior, experienced in ways he had never imagined.

OPERATION MARKET GARDEN, DAY 8:

Arnhem – Sunday, September 24, 1944

On September 24th, XXX Corps planned a last-ditch effort, which many considered an attempt to save-face. The plan was to cross the Neder Rijn and counter-attack the German forces surrounding the surviving soldiers of 1ˢᵗ Airborne Division. The plan seemed shaky from the beginning, but Horrocks and Browning approved the plan despite having many gaps and unanswered questions. Meanwhile, General Urquhart sent Colonel Warrack to meet with the German Medical Officer to propose a temporary ceasefire to evacuate the wounded back to safer areas in German territory. German commanders, Bittrich and Harzer, met Warrack and agreed to the ceasefire, while also providing Warrack with morphine and other medical supplies. The ceasefire lasted for several hours. Both sides helped to evacuate the wounded. The temporary cease fire also gave Dutch civilians an opportunity to escape the 'pocket of death' in Arnhem. Urquhart did not want to demonstrate weakness by requesting the cease fire, but he had no other option. Like a shark with blood in the water, the Germans sensed weakness, and they knew victory was within their grasp. At one point, the German officers begged Colonel Warrack to surrender, citing the number of wounded. 'Warrack listened in silence then shook his head slowly and said calmly, 'No. We have not come to surrender. We have come to fight' (Beevor 312). After approximately four hours, the ceasefire came to an end, and the explosions began once again. Some soldiers had the opportunity to catch a few hours of sleep for the first time in eight days. Others couldn't even close their eyes, because the silence felt deafening.

Later that night, the Dorsets and Polish Parachute Brigade attempted the planned river crossing. Only a few dozen soldiers made it across, while the majority of boats sank, resulting in hundreds of casualties. Early on the morning of September 25th, the operation was cancelled, and the final decision was made to evacuate the remnants of 1st Airborne Division. 'Operation Berlin' was hastily planned and would be executed that night.

OPERATION MARKET GARDEN, DAY 9:

Arnhem – Monday, September 25, 1944

For the evacuation, Urquhart developed a carefully articulated plan given the circumstances. On the evening of September 25th, once darkness descended upon Arnhem, the remaining soldiers in the division would withdraw to the riverbank, following white tape set by Engineers to mark the evacuation route. A rear guard would secure the flanks until the division was evacuated across the river. Boats would be waiting to ferry the weary paratroopers across until dawn, hopefully evading German detection. Urquhart's objective was to evacuate all remaining 1st Division soldiers.

That night, the skies opened up, and heavy rain made visibility very difficult for the evacuating soldiers. Finally catching a break, the rain also helped to cover their withdrawal. It took several hours for Rod and George to reach the riverbank. Once they did, they crouched along the bank in the mud and prayed for the incoming artillery rounds to miss for just a few more hours. The men were instructed not to fire any shots and to move as quietly as possible. They were told to avoid alerting the Germans of their evacuation, and one slip-up could place the entire evacuation in jeopardy. The first boats arrived at 2140 (9:40 PM), and the evacuation began. Soldiers used their hands, weapons, and any other 'oar-like' object to help paddle the boats. Other soldiers decided to try their luck at swimming across the wide river. Several made it, but many drowned or were washed downstream. Rod patiently waited for his turn. Eventually, Rod and 1,741 men from the 1st Airborne Division were successfully evacuated that night. The others were wounded, captured, or killed, with a few escaping in subsequent nights. A few soldiers, exhausted from lack of sleep, had fallen asleep during the cease fire and slept all the way through the evacuation. They woke up to find themselves alone behind enemy lines. Once the sun began to rise, the Germans became aware of the withdrawal and angry, they began firing as much artillery as they could muster. The rear guard was captured, along with remaining soldiers who couldn't make it across. For the next few days, 'Dead English soldiers drifted down the Neder Rijn. The boys hauled them out of the water with boat hooks, and pulled them on to the bank, where they were collected by the Red Cross to be buried in civilian cemeteries. It became a routine' (Beevor 333).

Rod tells his story of the evacuation day, 'After many days of fighting, the Germans slowly pushed us out of Arnhem, destroying the city along the way. On September 25th, we received an order from one of the officers to withdraw to a house three-four miles away. George Joy and I moved together as a team, and eventually we made it back to the farmhouse. It was a beautiful old stone farmhouse. There were hundreds of wounded soldiers laid out inside the house in addition to people like me, who were considered walking-wounded. We were so tired. Nine days of fighting. We were only supposed to be on that bridge for three days, and they were supposed to relieve us. None of us had slept. We set up a defensive perimeter around the farmhouse. Later that night, we received word that the Americans were coming to extract us. The guys sent to extract us swam across the Rhine River and told us they were going to send boats to pick us up that night. Later that night, we moved to the river carrying the wounded and the boats met us to carry us back across the Rhine. Once we made it across, they loaded us in trucks and transported us back to a medical facility.'

Silence descended on Arnhem for the first time in nine days. The Germans had expected XXX Corps to attack, but instead, 1st Airborne Division was evacuated and evaded complete destruction. The remaining wounded and captured paratroopers continued to display their pride and swagger to the Germans. 'A captured glider pilot, facing a panzergrenadier who was pointing a Mauser rifle at his chest, took a small mirror from his pocket to examine the growth of his beard. With a straight face, he asked his captor whether there was a dance in town that night' (Beevor 336).

At this point, Rod looked at me with a mischievous grin, and said, 'I have a funny story to tell you.' Amazed that he could find humor in this horrible situation, I replied, 'Please!' He began, 'We finally arrived at a medical facility the doctors and medics had rigged up. We were filthy, absolutely filthy, after fighting for eight days. This nurse came in, asked me to take my clothes off, and began washing me. So, I'm standing there, bare-ass naked, and she's about twenty-two years old and drop dead gorgeous. I'm only seventeen, so what happened? It stood up! [I'm now laughing hysterically, and I said to him, 'Apparently you weren't THAT tired!']. She looked at me with a smile, and said, 'Oh Rod.' She dipped the sponge in alcohol, rubbed it on my stomach wound, and [with an accompanying hand motion] it went right back down!'

After receiving medical treatment, the British Army evacuated Rod to Great Britain for a short period of leave. Rod was transported home in a medium-sized transport boat. To add insult to injury, aside from being wounded in combat, the trip home seemed to bother Rod more than his combat injury. 'It was so damn rough,' Rod explained with a nervous smile. 'We were in the North Sea, headed for Hull [located on the east coast of Great Britain]. What should have been a twelve-hour trip took two days. The damn boat would go up like this,' as Rod motioned with his hands. 'Then it would come down and we would all fall to the side. I was in the first boat. They have these big holds with large planks that cover the holds. A huge wave came over the bow of the ship and smashed the cover over the hold. I was down in the hold sitting on the edge of the staircase. Water came rushing into the hold knocking people over everywhere. People were vomiting everywhere, and now the vomit was in the water washing all over the place. Oh God, what a mess! I was thinking that I made it through all the crap in Arnhem and now I'm going to die going home!'

At this point, Rod abruptly pauses and says, 'Let me ask you a question.' I responded, 'Yes, sir.' Rod then quickly replied, 'Don't call me sir! Remember, I was only a private.' I laughed and explained that anyone who experienced Arnhem deserves to be called 'sir.' Rod thought for a moment then asked me, 'Did you have any fear of death?'

Without hesitation, I responded, 'Absolutely. Of course.' I explained the number of casualties we experienced during Operation Iraqi Freedom. I also explained what I did as a platoon leader. Once Rod found out I had been a lieutenant, he laughed and said, 'I'm surprised you made it out alive!' We then discussed the attrition rates for lieutenants and line officers in World War II. Platoon leaders were usually among the first to become casualties as they led their troops into combat. I explained to Rod, 'While being paralyzed at first, after a while, our minds became accustomed to the combat, and it was much easier to deal, almost routine. Regardless of how routine the attacks became, however, any soldier who tells you he wasn't scared is lying.' I described how the number of attacks consistently increased during our tour [we averaged four per day across our battalion's area of operations]. I also told Rod a story about a new platoon leader who had just arrived in our unit. I was training him to take over my platoon, and during his first mission, we were attacked by an RPG shooter from our right flank. The gunner on my vehicle was wounded, and when he fell down from the gunner's the hatch, the new platoon leader froze. He didn't know what to do. He was looking around, pale, with his mouth open. I snatched the radio hand-mike from his grasp and called in the attack. This was a typical reaction for someone who has never experienced combat. I'm sure I did the same thing during my first attack. Over time, the new lieutenant also became immune to the chaos.

Rod listened to my story intently, then responded, 'I remember, I was absolutely terrified. I think anyone who says they weren't scared is lying. I wasn't so much scared of dying. I was more scared of being so badly wounded that I could no longer live an independent life.'

OPERATION MARKET GARDEN

Conclusion

I asked Rod for his feelings as one of the approximately 1,500 British paratroopers who survived Arnhem. He said he felt proud, but he also felt significant feelings of anger toward Field Marshall Montgomery and the other commanders who placed his division in that difficult situation.

Beevor describes the 1st Airborne survivors as they arrived at the aid station following their evacuation from Arnhem: 'Captain Robert Franco, the surgeon in the 82nd Airborne, happened to see survivors of 1st Airborne as they reached Nijmegen. 'One look at them told the story,' he said. The American lieutenant Paul Johnson had been there when the first survivors began to arrive in the early hours. 'First, they were given a shot of rum, then some hot food and tea, and after eating they went to a long table of clerks, gave their name, rank and organization and were assigned to a bed for the night and as much morrow as they wanted. What a crew they were: dirty, wet, unshaven and haggard yes, but not cowed or defeated. Their spirit was wonderful, as was their discipline. Even those who had lost all their clothes in the river did not try to hurry past the others and get quickly into a warm bed' (338).

'The survivors from the division were billeted in three red-brick school buildings in Nijmegen. Many tried to make the best of the food, hot tea, and beds on offer. Some slept for forty-eight hours. Others were in a form of shock from their losses. 'Someone walked around asking 'Where's the 1st Battalion?' and a corporal, with tears in his eyes, answering 'This is it." Near him stood a handful of bedraggled men.' So few men appeared from the Light Regiment that Gunner Christie also 'felt like crying.' Hackett's 4th Parachute Brigade was reduced to 9 officers and 260 soldiers from more than 2,000' (Beevor 339). Rod's battalion was reduced to just a handful of soldiers.

Many Dutch citizens were executed for assisting the Allies. 'Along with the heroism displayed by our soldiers, it's also important for us to remember the sacrifices of the Dutch,' Rod said. The remaining Dutch citizens were forced to evacuate Arnhem after staying home through such difficult circumstances. Meanwhile, Germans looted and burned the remainder of the town to the ground. The Dutch had grown so accustomed to such horrors, they didn't bat an eye at the carnage around them. 'At one moment a mother saw her little son staring at a corpse which had been blown in two. She was terrified that he would be traumatized by the sight, but he turned to her, pointed down and said, 'Look, Mummy, half a man.' He then stepped over the corpse and walked on with a stick and handkerchief over his shoulder' (Beevor 347).

From November 1944, to May 1945, the Dutch experienced what became known as 'The Hunger Winter.' In addition to 180,000 Dutch citizens forced from their homes, there were 3,600 estimated Dutch civilian deaths through the course of Operation Market Garden. Thousands of Dutch civilians were sent to Germany to work in forced labor camps. The Germans seized all available food from the Dutch, particularly in the larger cities of The Hague, Rotterdam, and Amsterdam. They seized grain, eggs, dairy products and livestock, leaving sugar beets and tulip bulbs as the primary means of survival for the Dutch during the winter of 1944-45. Civilians were left to forage in the farmland for anything edible, and combined with an unusually harsh winter, there was simply no food to be found.

Typhoid and diphtheria epidemics spread due to the non-existent immune systems of the malnourished Dutch. Most adults lost one-third or more of their body weight. The dead were laid in the streets and taken to the cemetery every day by bicycle-led trailers. The Germans also confiscated the majority of Dutch vehicles for their own use, so it was difficult to transport any food into the cities. Food was only available on the black market and most Dutch civilians could not afford the prices. Eventually, Allied forces helped distribute limited amounts of food, but not enough to curb the crisis. More than 20,000 Dutch citizens perished from starvation alone, and many thousands more from the diseases and side effects resulting from starvation. Yet, through these horrible circumstances, the Dutch continued to display a loyalty to the Allies. They did not regret assisting Allied Forces during Operation Market Garden and beyond. Eventually Arnhem was rebuilt after Amsterdam adopted the city. Local craftsman worked for many years, completing the rebuild in 1969.

On October 8th, Allied bombers destroyed the Arnhem Bridge, which closed the book on one of the most unfortunate Allied missions in World War II. The same bridge that Rod, George, Lieutenant Colonel Frost, and thousands of paratroopers fought so bravely to hold, the Allies destroyed with one swift bombing mission. 'The failure of Operation Market Garden caused the Allies to abandon the idea of crossing the Rhine in the Netherlands. They switched the focus of their planning to Germany, as unbeknownst to the Allies at the time, Hitler was in the midst of planning his final great offensive later known as 'The Battle of the Bulge" (Beevor 362).

The men of the 1st British Airborne Division will forever be remembered as some of the bravest and most determined War Fighters of all-time. Winston Churchill displayed great passion when referencing the heroic deeds of the division. Within the British ranks, however, the blame game commenced. None of Britain's senior military leaders wanted to take responsibility for failure of the overall mission. Some leaders even convinced themselves that the mission had been a success. Beevor provides an outstanding synopsis of the overall mission:

> *Even allowing for the usual compulsion to put on the best face after a debacle, the self-congratulation and buck-passing among senior Allied commanders was bewildering. General Brereton claimed in October that 'Despite the failure of Second Army to get through to Arnhem and establish a permanent bridgehead over the Neder Rijn, Operation Market Garden was a brilliant success.' The implication was that any blame must lie with Horrocks and XXX Corps, not with the First Allied Airborne Army.*

> *Horrocks, in turn blamed Urquhart and his men. 'The 1st Airborne Division plan was fundamentally unsound and it fought a bad battle,' he said after the war. 'They did not know how to fight as a division.' Dempsey also blamed Urquhart's plan, still unaware that Brereton and Major General Williams had left him little alternative. The 1st Airborne 'had little chance of success because their own plan was so bad,' he said. It 'was not a good division, as a division. The men were gallant enough but they were not skilled tactically and they didn't know how to fight a regular battle once they were on the ground.' Urquhart, as one would have expected, did not blame anyone and did not rock the boat. He ended his report thus: 'Operation Market was not 100% a success and did not quite end as was intended. The losses were heavy, but all ranks appreciate that the risks involved were reasonable. There is no doubt that all would willingly undertake another operation under similar conditions in the future. We have no regrets.'*

> *Montgomery had been determined to bring the Allied air forces to heel by imposing his plan, apparently unaware*

that they, not he, had the final say. Then Browning, who had at last been given the field command he longed for, did nothing when faced with Major General Williams's refusal to allow his aircraft near the Arnhem and Nijmegen bridges. This eliminated any hope of surprise, the only advantage enjoyed by lightly armored airborne forces. Even Brereton's headquarters later admitted that 'The time between landing and getting into position was relatively long – between two and three hours [in fact closer to six hours]. Thereby the advantage of surprise at Arnhem was lost.' And Williams, with some justification, rejected the idea of two lifts in a day, which offered the only chance of delivering sufficient forces to their objectives. So, Browning must bear a large proportion of the blame because he failed to go straight back to Montgomery and insist that, with these limitations, the whole operation should be reconsidered.

In fact, the fundamental concept of Operation Market Garden defied military logic because it made no allowance for anything to go wrong, nor for the enemy's likely reactions. The most obvious response would have been for the Germans to blow up the bridges at Nijmegen, and it was only Model's own defiance of military logic which allowed Market Garden its sole hope of success. All the other deficiencies which emerged, such as bad communications and lack of ground-air liaison, simply compounded the central problem. In short, the whole operation ignored the old rule that no plan survives contact with the enemy. Such hubris always seemed to provoke Murphy's Law. As Shan Hackett indeed said much later, 'Everything that could go wrong did go wrong.'

Montgomery blamed weather, not the plan. He even as-

serted at one point that the operation had been 90 percent success, since they had got nine-tenths of the way to Arnhem. This prompted the scorn of Air Chief Marshal Arthur Tedder, Eisenhower's deputy, who observed, 'one jumps off a cliff with an even higher success rate, until the last few inches.' Prince Bernhard, on hearing of Montgomery's optimistic assessment of the battle, is said to have remarked, 'My country cannot afford another Montgomery victory.' But at least the field marshal issued a well-deserved tribute to the 1st Airborne Division. In an open letter which he gave to Urquhart as he was about to fly back to England, he finished: 'In years to come it will be a great thing for a man to be able to say: "I fought at Arnhem."'

The Germans analyzed the British failure with acute professional interest, especially the way they lost 'Uberraschungserfolg' – 'the effect of surprise.' The great flaw in the plan at Arnhem, as Oberstleutnant von der Heydte pointed out later, was that the British paratrooper brigade that landed on the first day was not strong enough and that forces were not dropped on both sides of the river. 'They made an astounding mess of things at Arnhem,' he concluded. Both German and Dutch officers disagreed with Williams's claim that the south bank of the Neder Rijn near the bridge was unsuitable for gliders and paratroops. And the strength of the flak batteries was grossly exaggerated, as Generaloberst Student pointed out. As a result, he added, the British lost 'surprise, the strongest weapon of airborne troops. At Arnhem, the enemy didn't play this trump card and it cost him the victory.' Bittirch, who had had great respect for Montgomery's generalship up until then, changed his opinion after Arnhem.

> *To expect Horrock's XXX Corps to advance from the Meuse-*
> *Escaut Canal, just inside Belgium, for 103 kilometers along*
> *a single road to Arnhem simply asked for trouble. Even*
> *with air superiority, it was exactly the sort of action*
> *which the German general staff would have dismissed as a*
> *'Husarenstuck' – 'an ill-thought-out cavalry raid'. The rate*
> *of advance required did not allow for any hold-up's. And*
> *despite mounting evidence to the contrary, Montgomery*
> *still believed that the Germans would be incapable of re-*
> *acting rapidly to form an effective defense. General David*
> *Fraser, who as a Grenadier subaltern took part in the battle*
> *for Nijmegen, wrote later, 'Operation Market Garden was,*
> *in an exact sense, futile. It was a thoroughly bad idea, badly*
> *planned and only – tragically – redeemed by the outstanding*
> *courage of those who executed it' (364-366).*

Montgomery later blamed Eisenhower's headquarters for lack of proper support, which infuriated Eisenhower's staff. Montgomery blamed everyone possible to avoid placing a dark cloud over his generalship. Meanwhile, the surviving soldiers of the British 1st Airborne Division 'took no further part in the war until the time of German surrender in May 1945, they were flown to Norway to disband the 350,000 Germans still there. The division was officially disbanded in August' (Beevor 369).

To this day, the Dutch people display a deep affection for the brave Allies who came to rescue them. My friend Herman, Rod's neighbor, was born in the Netherlands. Maureen recalls a story shortly after they became neighbors. Herman walked up to Rod with tears in his eyes, hugged Rod, and thanked him. All Rod could ask was, 'How can you thank me? Your town was destroyed. It was horrible.' Herman replied, 'It was worth it. You came to help us, and that's all that matters.' Herman's message of thanks has been echoed for many years by the Dutch. Although their country was ravaged, they fought valiantly alongside the Allies, and as a result, a bond was formed that can never be broken.

While Rod's adventures in Europe were far from finished, he never again faced combat like he experienced in Arnhem. 'It was absolutely brutal,' Rod said. 'I never experienced anything like that again, and I pray that nobody ever will.' Rod does not like Field Marshall Montgomery, but he also doesn't harbor any ill-will toward his commanders. He doesn't believe they intended to send them into a death trap – only that they exhibited poor leadership during the planning phase of the operation. I understand where Rod is coming from. As line soldiers, we are given missions. We are expected to have confidence that proper planning has occurred. We MUST have confidence in our leaders and their ability to plan a successful operation. When executing a mission that is poorly planned, the soldiers on the line are the ones who suffer. Men like Rod are left to deal with the ineptitude of the planners and their attempts to turn lemons into lemonade. Regardless of how history judges Operation Market Garden, the heroism exhibited by Rod and his fellow soldiers can NEVER be understated. They faced impossible odds and never gave up. The swagger and determination they exhibited was among the greatest in military history.

ROD'S MILITARY SERVICE

Post-Arnhem

D ue to Rod's injury and decimation of his unit, the British Command removed Rod from his Commando Regiment and transferred him to the Dorset Regiment, along with fellow Commandoes who survived Operation Market Garden [approximately 40 of them]. They were allowed to continue wearing their Commando berets and badges, which caused Rod to feel a bit out of place in his new unit.

After spending a week recovering in Britain, Rod returned to France and joined his new regiment on their advance into Germany. The Dorset Regiment, formally known as the 'Dorsetshire Regiment,' was formed in 1881. Rich in history, the Dorset's, as they're known, served heroically in World War I, the Anglo-Irish War, the Malabar Campaign and of course, World War II. In World War II, the Dorset's served valiantly at Dunkirk, the D-Day Invasion, crossing of the Rhine, and many other battles along their advance from France into Germany.

As members of the Dorset Regiment, Rod and his fellow Commando soldiers struggled to fit in. Rod didn't know exactly why. 'Perhaps it was because they let us wear our Commando patches or berets, or perhaps it was because they thought we were given special treatment,' Rod explained. 'They didn't know what we had been through, and none of us really cared to talk about it.'

One of Rod's most difficult (and vivid) memories came toward the end of the war. As the Dorset Regiment moved into North Germany and into the Belsen area [today known as Lower Saxony in northern Germany], they became one of the first Allied units to discover the Bergen-Belsen [commonly known as 'Belsen'] Concentration Camp. Belsen was one of the first Nazi Concentration Camps to be liberated by Allied Forces after Germany surrendered.   The Bergen-Belsen camp was originally established as a Prisoner of War (POW) Camp in the late 1930's to house Soviet prisoners. In 1943, parts of the camp were converted into a concentration camp, and soon, disease [typhus, typhoid fever, tuberculosis], and starvation ravaged the camp. It is estimated that 120,000 prisoners passed through the camp, and due to the destruction of the files by SS personnel, only about half of the prisoners are known by name. It is estimated that more than 50,000 people [primarily Jews, Czech's, Poles, Anti-Nazi Christians, Homosexuals, and Gypsies] died at the camp.

When Rod arrived, it was a horrible scene. There were 60,000 prisoners at the camp, and they were dying at a rate of five hundred per day. The prisoners were starving and had not been provided food or water for days. There were 13,000 bodies lying in trenches, many decomposing in full view. Anne Frank and her sister Margot were among those bodies. Anne (at the age of 15) and Margot both died in February 1945, just a few months before the camp was liberated, by Rod and other British soldiers. The camp was well-documented after its discovery and became one of the primary symbols of Nazi horrors that took place during World War II. Allied Forces (and therefore the American and British people) did not understand the full extent of the German atrocities being committed at the Concentration Camps until they were actually discovered.

'They never told us about anything like this. I've never seen anything like it in my life,' Rod said. 'We walked over the hill and saw a large fence with concertina wire on top of it. All of these people were standing up against the fence, and they were so skinny.' Rod paused for a moment and looked down before he continued. 'So skinny,' he said again slowly. 'You could see the outline of bones under their skin. Their bellies were all sticking out. They looked at us with blank stares, as if they weren't even alive. We continued to patrol past the main entrance, and we saw huge fields with massive trenches, stacked full of bodies.' Rod paused again before continuing. 'Stacks of bodies,' he repeated. 'To this day, I can close my eyes and see them as clearly as the day I was there. It was horrible, the worst thing I've ever seen. Like Zombies. The smell. Oh God, the smell. It was absolutely horrible.'

In early-1945, defeat was inevitable for Nazi Germany, as the Allies continued to encircle Berlin. The war was coming to an end, which made Rod very happy, but there were still isolated skirmishes, usually initiated by the SS (Schutzstaffel) and other hardline Nazi's. Rod said, 'Our nerves were always quite raw, even as the war drew to a close. One night, we were guarding an ammunition point, which consisted of large boxes outside of a church. Our squad of six soldiers decided to rotate through the church to sleep during the night. Two of us would stand guard while the other four slept. In the middle of the night while I was sleeping, one of the sentries on-duty fired two shots and screamed, 'They're in the cemetery across the street!' So, the four of us woke up, grabbed our weapons and headed to the cemetery, where we fanned out to identify and destroy the Germans. As we entered the cemetery, the moon cast just enough light for me to see a large figure. I began to fire at the big German. Bullets started ricocheting all over the place, and we took cover. Finally, we ceased fire and using our lanterns [big flashlights], we illuminated the target. Upon closer inspection, I discovered that I had shot the hell out of a full-size angel! It gave us all a light-hearted moment.'

Rod vividly remembers a variety of interesting stories that took place as Allied forces transitioned from an invasion force to an occupation force following Germany's surrender on May 7, 1945.

After the war, Rod and his fellow soldiers were forced to deal heavily in the black market to obtain basic necessities for their new occupation force in Germany. One day, the regimental commander assembled the entire regiment into one massive formation. The commander, using a megaphone, stated the following, 'It has been brought to my attention by the war office that they're having some trouble in the Middle East, in Palestine. I would like to ask for volunteers to go there to assist in the region. You will be given new uniforms and new weapons. All volunteers, please step forward.'

'Not a soul moved,' Rod said. 'Not one person! They were addressing a bunch of combat Veterans, and we just finished having the shit kicked out of us. Who in their right mind would volunteer to go to the Middle East?' Thankfully, Rod was not selected for that duty assignment.

Next, the regimental commander sent Rod's battalion to Nuremburg for a two-week assignment. 'I was one of the guards who patrolled the outside perimeter during the famous Nuremburg Trials. A funny story: One of the Germans tried to escape out of the bathroom, so the guard immediately shot him. The guard reacted quickly and down the German went.' Rod pauses for a second then chuckles, 'They [his commander] sent him to France for a one-week vacation to Paris!' Rod laughed again then said, 'After that, we all hoped the prisoners would try to escape on our watch!'

Rod's expression grew serious, and he said, 'You know, when we were at Nuremburg, I really felt sorry for some of the Germans. I often saw them being taken to be hung. They would walk right past where we were standing on guard duty. That has to be a horrible feeling. It was winter with lots of snow on the ground, and they were wearing very light clothes, like pajamas, walking through the snow on the way to the gallows. My wife asked why I felt sorry for them, and I told her that I feel sorry for anyone who is about to die.'

'They sent my battalion to Brunswick,' Rod explained. 'Nice town with a really nice airfield. I found a car there,' as Rod laughed for a moment and shook his head. Rod became the driver for one of the lieutenants. He loved this assignment. 'It was truly an easy job. I was attached to the MT unit, called the Motor Transportation unit. The lieutenant was engaged to a German woman. After the engagement party, he insisted on driving back to our base. There was a flat-bed semi parked in the road. He didn't see it in-time and we ran straight into it. It killed the lieutenant instantly and pinned me inside. It took them four hours to cut me out, and I had a bunch of broken ribs.'

Rod was also stationed in Berlin, where his unit resided at Olympia Stadium, one of a few structures in Berlin not destroyed during the war. Upon Germany's surrender, the Allies divided the city into four zones: British, Russian, French, and American. He tells a hilarious story of going out in Berlin with four buddies and getting drunk. Apparently, they had a grand time. In the morning, they woke up confused and disoriented. Rod asked aloud, 'Where the hell are we?' Soon, they figured out they were right in the middle of the Russian zone.

In Berlin, Rod was assigned to a logistics team responsible for procuring and distributing supplies to Allied Forces across Europe. He (and a group of soldiers) would travel abroad in trains, picking up supplies, which included procurement on the Black Market when necessary. 'The trains were huge,' Rod explained. 'More than a mile long. One day, we traveled into Russia, just a few miles from Stalingrad. We weren't actually inside of Stalingrad, but we were close enough to see the remains of the city after the battles. They lost more than a million men in Stalingrad. More than a million Russian soldiers died. Stalingrad held long enough for them to build this huge Army, which they used to surround and ultimately defeat the Germans.' On his trip to Russia, the train had to cross the Elbe River on a mile-long Bailey Bridge constructed by U.S. Army Engineers. As they approached the bridge,

Rod could see the Russians had disassembled the Bailey bridge and constructed their own wooden version. Rod said, 'Boy it sure didn't look like it would hold the weight of our train. The five of us ended up getting off the train and walking across. The driver of the train didn't seem excited about crossing either, but he did. Luckily the bridge held!' Rod and his fellow soldiers transported food, medical supplies and other items to troops across Europe. Basically, they were the Amazon.com of today.

Rod told another story about that same trip: 'George Joy, my buddy, who I served with through my entire time in the Army, was one lucky son-of-a-bitch. He was never wounded, never scratched. When we crossed the Elb, we were sitting on the train looking out over the countryside. George saw a fisherman off in the distance. George said, 'Watch this,' and he grabbed his Enfield rifle. I yelled, 'George, no! You're going to kill him.' George replied, 'No, I'm not,' and he fired a few shots out in front of the fisherman. The fisherman saw the bullets and ran like hell!' Rod and George couldn't stop laughing. 'The things that we find funny in war,' Rod said quietly.

Rod participated in these supply runs for three-to-four months. He laughed as he explained his aptitude in black market operations. 'We were stationed in Berlin at Olympiastadion [Olympic Stadium]. We used to pick up the trains at the Rail Yard. It was HUGE! We traveled to quite a few places, and we were usually able to find whatever we were looking for. Then, we would sell it on the black market. It was a quite a business,' Rod said with a smile.

Rod explained that in Berlin at the time, money was completely worthless. After Allied Forces captured the German treasury reserves, German currency had no value (similar to our capture of Saddam's reserves in Iraq). 'German money was worthless, but cigarettes were very valuable,' Rod explained. 'You could buy anything you wanted with cigarettes. I didn't smoke, but I made a lot of money with cigarettes. I would trade cans of 50 cigarettes at a time. At one point, I had a whole suitcase full of German money, and it was all absolutely worthless. I didn't know at first, but I soon learned, and I learned the hard way. I needed to procure goods, not money.'

Another story Rod remembers: 'The Army informed me that I had six months before demobbing. 'Demobbed' was [and still is] a term we used to describe the end of Army service, or the time that I would become a civilian again [similar to the acronym 'ETS' in the US Military]. They sent my battalion to Austria, and I was responsible for driving the water wagon. They were driving 30 mph in the front, and I was in the back driving 60 mph to keep up! We had to drive through the French Alps, which were absolutely stunning. We drove up steep mountains with slopes like this,' as Rod demonstrated the slope of the mountains with his right arm. 'And no guard rails,' Rod continued. 'Every time I'd drive around a bend, the water would slosh to the left or right, and I felt like the entire truck was going to tip right over the edge, thousands of feet down,' and Rod laughed. 'We finally arrived at Klagenfurt, Austria. From there you could see all the way to Italy. We were there in the winter, and it was a big ski area. I had never skied before. I bought a pair of long wooden skis on the black market, and I decided to give it a try. I couldn't ski for anything. I kept crossing my skis and falling down the hill. One day, a young boy [as Rod motions a height of about four feet with his hand] with short little skis comes flying by me down the slope, back and forth, like a professional skier. He skied up to me and said excitedly, 'Tommy, Tommy, Tommy.'' Rod paused for a second to explain that Tommy was the slang used by the locals to identify British soldiers. 'The little boy said, 'Tommy, if you give me a cigarette, I'll teach you to ski,' Rod laughed and continued, 'I told the boy, you're too small to have a cigarette! The boy responded and said, 'No I'm not.' So, I gave him a cigarette and the boy gave me lessons for the rest of the afternoon. Eventually I picked it up. Once I learned, I had a ball!'

Rod was stationed in Austria for the next several months. Eventually, he returned to Britain where he was officially discharged from the British Armed Forces.

POST-MILITARY LIFE

After Rod was discharged from military service, he returned home. There was nothing for him there. His mother had died in 1945, and his father wasn't around much, so Rod felt it was time to build his own life. At the age of fourteen, with the assistance of Rod's father, Rod had been 'indentured' to British Power Boats as part of a seven-year manufacturing apprentice program. Growing up as an American kid, Maureen [Rod's wife] finds the idea of this program horrifying. 'It was like they were being sold,' she said. The apprenticeship covered all different types of manufacturing. Rod was rotated to different facilities and manufacturing plants where he learned a variety of technical and engineering skills. During the first year, he was paid two shillings per week, the equivalent of twenty cents (USD) per week. Each year during the apprenticeship, his weekly pay increased by one shun. His service in the Army counted toward his seven years, so by the time Rod was discharged, he only owed one more year. He served the remaining year with Harland & Wolff [a successful British company still in business today], where they eventually terminated Rod following the completion of the seven-year obligation for his apprenticeship [customary for that type of program]. Rod remembers working on big ships making huge, heavy round pipes, more than four feet in diameter using heavy flat stock. 'I thought to myself, there has to be better way to make a living,' Rod said with a smile.

Rod traveled up to Basingstoke, north of Winchester, where railway trains were manufactured in Britain. Rod thought about seeking employment, but when he looked around, he didn't prefer the type of heavy assembly work they were doing. He said, 'it was worse than the British shipyards,' still grinning. Rod tried to seek re-employment with British Power Boats, but they had shut down operations from lack of business after the war. It was a tough economy for Britain after the war, with thousands of prior-service members seeking employment, Rod was offered another job with Harland & Wolff, which he really wanted. Unfortunately, he was laid off again during a lull in business between ships. Rod continued to seek employment, and eventually he landed a job with Folland Aircraft, located just fifteen miles from where he grew up in Southampton. 'I didn't move back home, because there wasn't much for me there. Dad eventually moved back in, and Tony lived there for a while, but it wasn't the same without my mom,' Rod explained. Folland Aircraft was (and still is) an aircraft manufacturing company that specialized in building the 'Gnat' Aircraft. 'It was a very different type of airplane that's still in production today,' Rod described. 'The left wing is interchangeable with the right wing, and so forth. All of the parts are modular and interchangeable. I participated in the development of the aircraft. They originally hired me to assist with copper-smithing, a skill that I learned during my seven-year apprenticeship.'

Rod continued his story: 'There was a two-inch aluminum pipe, and the pipe had to have five bends in it, shaped like this,' as Rod demonstrates a curving pipe with his hands. 'Nobody could figure out how to manufacture it, so they asked me if I could take a shot. They were paying one pound per pipe at the time, which was about four U.S. dollars. I looked at it and thought, 'There's no way I can make that pipe.' I had learned similar skills during my apprenticeship at British Power Boats, so I decided to give it my best shot. I went to the wood pattern shop, or whatever you want to call it, and I asked them to make me a wooden duplicate of the pipe. After that, I created a kirksite casting from the wood pipe in two halves. Next, I filled up the pipe with sand and used an OTTO

[hand] press. I pushed the press down, and when I opened up the die, it was a perfect pipe. Absolutely perfect. So, I thought, 'Oh, I'm going to make some money here!' And I did! When I submitted my design, they sent it all the way up to management. Management asked how I was the only one who could figure out how to make this pipe. I was immediately promoted to process engineer sent to the hangar where the Gnat was being developed. The hanger was brand new, built specifically for the Gnat program. I worked there for about a year helping to develop the aircraft. It was a fun job, and I learned a lot.' After his promotion, Folland Aircraft increased Rod's salary to 900 pounds per year, a large sum of money during that period in Great Britain. World War II had broken the country, and it took Great Britain many years for its economy to recover.

Rod enjoyed riding motorcycles, so he [and three other partners] decided to open their own motorcycle factory. Given Rod's technical skills, he felt opening a business would be a surefire way to make lots of money. 'That didn't last long,' Rod said with a smile. They operated out of a building the size of a four-car garage. The garage had a small lathe, along with presses and other equipment. 'Right after we opened the business, American steel workers decided to go on strike, so we couldn't get steel! It was hard to manufacture motorcycles without steel,' Rod said. Rod and his partners had already purchased the machines needed, and thankfully, they found someone willing to purchase the fledgling business. One of his partners had a wealthy father who bought the business from Rod and the other partners. Years later, Rod's former company evolved into one of the largest producers of off-road vehicles in Europe. The boy's family is one of the most successful and wealthiest families today in the UK.

Rod was employed by Folland Aircraft for one year before Avro contacted him. Avro was a British company that built aircraft in Canada. Rod asked me if I knew about Avro, and at the time, I did not. Avro extended an offer Rod couldn't refuse, and soon, he moved to Toronto, Ontario. Rod's entire demeanor changed. I could see the excitement on Rod's face, and I could hear it in his voice, as Rod discussed his tenure at Avro. Once hired by Avro, Rod was assigned to Orenda, a subsidiary of Avro, to assist in the design of a new state-of-the-art jet engine, the 'Iroquois.' 'It was an amazing company,' Rod explained. 'My first job was to work on the Iroquois engine. The Iroquois was a state-of-the-art titanium jet engine, designed to propel fighter jets at speeds greater than Mach Two. The big fan jets that we have today were developed back then. Everything is made out of titanium now, but back then, the jets were all manufactured from iron castings. At the time, they didn't know how to make titanium molds. I worked and worked on this problem. Eventually I discovered that by exciting the titanium through rollers, the molecules would move, which allowed the titanium to be formed and molded. That solved a huge problem. Next, they asked if I could weld the titanium. I tried it, and no way, it didn't work. So, I created an automatic welder using a turn table and the welds were slightly better but still not good enough. A co-worker came up with the idea of changing the atmosphere. We created a bell-shaped object that we used to control atmospheric conditions around the weld. We experimented with the titanium welds by putting the pieces inside the bell, welding them, and eventually, they came out perfect! We didn't even have to grind them. From that particular experiment, the titanium welding technology was adapted all over the world. It is still used today.'

Palmiro Campagna, in his book *The Avro Arrow: For the Record*, provides a synopsis of the cutting-edge manufacturing techniques used to design the Iroquois engine. Rod played a significant role in the development of the welding and tooling techniques described by Campagna:

> *While other manufacturers were attempting to use titanium blades on already existing steel supports within an engine, Orenda [a subsidiary of Avro] elected to use titanium*

*in the Iroquois design from the outset; as a result, sup-
porting structures could also be made lighter. For example,
a steel supporting disc would have weighed forty-eight
pounds, whereas the titanium equivalent weighed in at sixteen pounds. Likewise, steel blades would weigh twenty-
nine pounds, compared to the titanium seventeen pounds.
Not only did the use of titanium allow for a lighter design,
working with titanium resulted in the development of new
techniques in welding and machining, putting Orenda at
the forefront of that technology as well (36).*

Avro's objective in developing the Iroquois was to manufacture
an engine capable of propelling Avro's new prototype CF-105
Arrow jet (discussed below) to speeds greater than Mach Two,
previously thought to be impossible. Avro also intended to
manufacture and sell the Iroquois to other Allied nations like the
United States. Rod played an instrumental role in the engineering
and development of this world-class jet engine. Without Rod's
engineering of the titanium molding and welding processes,
Mach Two would not have been possible at that time.

At Avro, Rod was assigned several other top-secret projects. First,
he worked on a flying saucer project, known years later as the
'Avrocar.' Flying saucers weren't just fictional spacecrafts in
movies. Rod, working with a team of engineers, developed a real-
life flying saucer. It was thirty feet in diameter (you can see a
picture on the internet), and the pilot sat in the middle of the
craft. 'It was supposed to travel 600 miles per hour,' Rod said with
a smile. 'But, in reality, it barely got off the ground!' After years
of development, Avro transported the flying saucer prototype to
Fort Eustis, Virginia for a test flight. It was only set up for one single pilot, and it hovered a few feet above the ground, but that was
the extent of it. 'It was uncontrollable,' Rod said. Hundreds of engineers worked on the project, and it ended up a complete failure.

The most exciting (and strangest) project Rod worked on was the legendary 'CF-105 Avro Arrow'. The Arrow was a fighter jet, generations ahead of its time and one of the fastest ever developed. 'In 1956, it flew Mach Two, unprecedented for that time. There were five prototypes manufactured,' Rod explained. 'It was the most beautiful plane I have ever seen. It blew windows out of buildings when it broke the sound barrier. Gorgeous plane.' Rod paused for a second. 'Now this is the weird part. I had already left Canada for the U.S. in 1956, and at that time, the Arrow factory was going full-steam ahead. Inexplicably, on a Friday night in 1959, a voice came over the loud-speaker. It said, 'As of tonight, this plant is closed, effective immediately. They closed the plant forever. Avro destroyed all five of the planes, the plans, paperwork, and everything associated with the project. It was the strangest thing I had ever heard of. Fourteen thousand people worked on the Arrow project, and it was shut down overnight.'

We pulled up a picture of the CF-105 Avro Arrow on the internet and passed it around. It really was a beautiful plane. It was the fastest supersonic jet aircraft built at the time. The Arrow was also the first plane to deploy a new type of missile/rocket deployment system with a larger payload of missiles. Rod remembered flight tests over Lake Ontario that would blow windows out of local homes from the sonic boom.

On February 20, 1959, the Arrow project was cancelled abruptly by Canadian Prime Minister John Diefenbaker. More than 25,000 employees lost their jobs [Approximately 14,000 worked directly for Avro, and others through contractors associated with the project]. It's still a mystery today as to why the project was cancelled. 'The fallout from the cancellation was enormous and extended far beyond the obviously significant loss of twenty-five thousand jobs. The *Financial Post* of September 20, 1958, published a list of businesses across Canada that would lose contracts as a result of the termination. The article stated that one hundred thousand Canadians would be affected, along with many new industries, particularly in the area of electronics' (Campagna 17).

Following the Arrow project cancellation, perhaps the most significant loss for Canada was the exodus of Canadian-born, technological talent. Avro had assembled one of the most-talented teams of aerospace engineers in the world, to that point. Overnight, aerospace engineers were suddenly un-employed and highly recruited by companies in other nations. Rod had already been recruited by General Motors, and now other engineers were heavily recruited by NASA. In fact, at least twenty-five former Avro engineers were hired by NASA and later led the development of the U.S. Space Program, including John Glenn's space capsule and the Gemini/Apollo programs. To this day, the Canadian aerospace program has not recovered from the mass-exodus of engineering talent in 1959. It could be argued that the cancellation of the Arrow program led to the United States solidifying its' position of dominance in aerospace engineering, still held by the U.S. today.

The Royal Canadian Air Force ended up purchasing American-made aircraft to build their fledgling Air Force and missile-defense programs. As recently as last year (2018), there have been calls for Canada to resume the Arrow program. Many people believe that the Avro was too expensive for Canada's limited Air Force budget at the time. There are many conspiracy theories related to the Arrow's cancellation, most notably that the U.S. government was behind the termination of the program. It will always remain a mystery, but to this day, the Arrow was one of the fastest and most powerful jets ever developed. Rod had the honor of working on the project.

Rod worked three years in Toronto for Avro. At that time, Rod received a recruitment letter from General Motors (GM). GM, one of the most sought-after companies in the world, offering Rod a position he couldn't refuse. GM invited Rod to Warren, Michigan for an interview and immediately GM offered Rod a position that nearly doubled his previous salary. Rod expected a slow transition, but just five weeks later, he moved to Detroit, Michigan and began working at the biggest plant he had ever seen. 'It was a one-square mile-wide factory, with beautiful gardens and huge buildings,' Rod explained. 'It housed one of the biggest wind tunnels in the United States, capable of blasting 200 mph wind. Three thousand engineers and scientists came together to create the wind tunnel.'

Rod loved his new job, and within one month of his employment, he had already been promoted. 'Then, I worked for a guy named Ehringer, and he kept telling me, 'Six more months of training,' then when I finished that, he told me I needed to train for six more months. Finally, I got out from underneath him and steadily advanced in the Chevy Engineering Center. On the GM campus there was also a division called Fisher Body. Fisher Body was a famous old carriage company (Fisher Brothers) from the turn of the century. Fisher Body had a one-million square foot facility. Huge. Overnight, they closed it down, renamed it the 'Headquarters Building,' and transferred me to this facility as the manager-in-charge of manufacturing. Suddenly, I had more than eight hundred people working for me. I guess I was just in the right place at the right time. I kept getting promoted,' Rod said with a chuckle. Knowing Rod and his work ethic today, it's easy to see why he was promoted so frequently. It didn't take long to understand that Rod possessed a very rare engineering aptitude, combined with an even rarer work ethic. Rod and I chuckled about his tenure in the Army as a Commando. With such a powerful engineering mind, imagine the possibilities if the military had employed Rod in such a capacity.

Next, Rod began telling the story of his role in the development of the Corvette. Yes, the Corvette. 'It was fantastic,' Rod said with a smile. Rod discussed Chevy's design and prototyping for the 1980 Corvette. 'The Chief Engineer [Rod pauses to recall his name] evaluated the point where the frame joined the fire wall and asked for my input. I examined it during the engineering mockup part of the project, and I told him, 'This isn't going to work. You have a sheer point and you need to cover that point.' The chief engineer told me that the computer had designed this car, and it was the first computer-designed car. Because a computer designed it, it would definitely work. Guess what? It didn't work,' Rod chuckled. For the 1982 Corvette, which was never actually manufactured, the chief engineer called Rod into his office and said, 'We want you to run the plastics department under your management.' Rod, said, 'okay,' as he asked himself, 'what the hell was one more department at that point?' GM challenged him with the project of simulating SMC [Sheet-Mold Compounds]. Rod replied, 'Okay, well how do I do that?' The engineer said, 'I don't know, it's never been done before.' At first Rod grew frustrated as he wondered why they had assigned him yet another impossible task. 'Why me?' he asked himself.

Rod began researching the subject. As he read about ship building in Holland, he discovered a man who manufactured fiberglass boats with 100-foot molds. The name of the company was listed on the back of the book, so Rod picked up the phone in Detroit and called the company in Holland. Eventually he tracked the man down. The gentleman told Rod, 'I know the problem you're having. You keep blowing the dyes apart, don't you?' Rod replied, 'You've got that right! The pressure is too great when we try to inject it.' The man replied, 'We found a solution. Every one-hundred millimeters square, we insert a drinking straw into the mold to alleviate the air pressure. As the liquid flows through, the resin flows up through the top of the straws and it continues to the next straw.' Rod, equipped with a new idea, decided to test the new technique. He asked his chief engineer to purchase a large press. It was a twelve-foot square press with a six-foot opening. It had six patterns inside. The entire department gathered as the new press operated for the first time, applying pressure to the different plates in sequence, alleviating pressure while applying it to other areas. When the press finished, the engineers stared with amazement, as a shiny, smooth door panel sat in front of them. The engineer, looking on with amazement, asked, 'Rod, do you think we can paint that while it's being formed in the mold?' Rod replied, 'I don't know, but we can try spraying a powder agent inside the mold, and we'll see what happens.' Rod laughs as he looked and me and exclaimed, 'It worked! I was absolutely amazed!'

Rod helped to invent yet another new manufacturing technique, SMC [sheet-molding compound], which was soon adapted across the auto industry. Large fiberglass molds, previously impossible to manufacture, became commonplace in the industry. Rod explained that the bodies for new vehicles today all use the SMC process. Rod wished he had invented the new technology himself. He paused and added how happy he was to develop this technology for General Motors [which patented the technology with 4 separate patents]. 'What a wonderful place to work,' he said twice with a nostalgic smile on his face. 'I had a wonderful life there. Even still today, it's a futuristic, wonderful place to work.' While Rod worked for GM, they provided him with an automobile of his choice, and it would always be a new car. He drove the latest and greatest vehicle, and GM covered his gas as well. To this day, Rod only drives GM vehicles. Currently, he drives a Chevy Volt, which he says is a wonderful car. He explained how it works: 'Each day, you plug it into a 110 outlet, and it gives you sixty-two miles per charge. That takes care of anything I need to do around here. If we take a longer trip, there is a nine-gallon gas tank, and the car gives you forty-two miles-per-gallon gas mileage.' He offered to take me for a ride, and he explained how fast it accelerated from zero to sixty miles per hour. 'It keeps up with the Corvette from zero to sixty,' Rod said with an excited grin on his face. 'That's what I really like about it!' I told Rod I would be honored to ride in his Chevy. Briefly, my mind flashed back to when my grandpa turned 90. He insisted on driving, and it was a bit scary riding with him as he aged. For some reason, I felt perfectly comfortable riding with Rod.

Rod also described a hydrogen-powered car in development at

GM, called the 'Snowburner', which would achieve more than 150 miles per gallon of gas. It was a big deal within GM, but one day it was mysteriously cancelled, never to be discussed again. Conspiracy theories surround the sudden disappearance of this ultra-efficient vehicle, but in Rod's words, 'we'll never know the truth, so there's no point in worrying about it.'

Rod retired from GM at age sixty. While Rod and Maureen lived in Michigan, they purchased a thirty-four-foot Cruiser boat, which they used to sail on the lake and rivers in the area. Prior to Rod's retirement, they made a plan to spend their retirement in Florida. Both Rod and Maureen decided they wanted to celebrate Rod's retirement by sailing from Detroit, Michigan, to their new home in Florida [a distance of more than 2,000 miles by sea]. They took a six-month vacation, weaving their way to the Atlantic Ocean and sailing down the east coast of the United States. They lived on a canal near Detroit. They sold their house, walked to their back yard, boarded their boat, and sailed off to Florida. The journey took them through the Erie Canal, down the Hudson River to the Atlantic Ocean, and south along the east coast, finally sailing around the southern tip of Florida. Rod tells me with a smile, 'Do you know that over 2,000 miles of sailing down south, we never once ran aground?' He pauses, then continues, 'Until we reached the bridge here, a mile from our house, and, boomp, we ran aground!' Rod jokes about his wife Maureen, who is fifteen years younger than him. She often tells Rod how much younger she is than him, but yet she can never keep up with him. I told Rod that he doesn't look or act like he's over ninety, so Maureen must be keeping him young. Or maybe he's keeping her young.

Hurricane Charley [which hit while I was in Iraq – I remember watching in horror from there] destroyed Rod's boat in 2004. 'Charley took care of my boat,' Rod said. 'My boat weighed 18,000 pounds. Charley picked it up out of its hoist, turned it on its side and destroyed it. So, I decided my boating days were over. and I bought a motor home.'

Rod took a financial hit when GM declared bankruptcy. He worked for years to accumulate quite a stockpile of GM stock. 'Overnight, the stock dropped from nearly $80/share to nothing,' Rod explains. 'I used to live like a hog, but as GM was going bankrupt, I lost our life and medical insurance, and quite a bit of money.' He looks at me and shrugs his shoulders, 'Oh well,' he laughs. 'Maureen and I are comfortable, and we live a great life.'

What else could I expect this amazing hero to say? This is a man who jumped into unspeakable danger seventy-five years ago and has accomplished impossible things in his life ever since.

Rod asked me what I did for a living, and I explained our real estate business. We laughed about managing rental properties, and Rod summed it up with one great point when said, 'What a pain in the ass they are.' He complimented my mom and said, 'What a lovely lady.' I told Rod that I didn't take after my mom in that regard, and that I inherited my father's stubbornness and temperament. I explained to Rod that the last thing I ever wanted to do growing up was join the military. Rod said that he felt the same way. Lo and behold, we both joined the military, and we both ended up going to war.

TODAY

Rod is a naturalized American citizen today. He's a dual citizen of Great Britain and the U.S. 'I absolutely love this country. It's such a wonderful place,' Rod said with an ear-to-ear grin on his face. 'I would fight for this country right now, the same way I fought for Britain.' Rod went on and on about his wonderful experiences in America. 'I've met so many wonderful people, and I've been to so many wonderful places,' Rod said. He paused for a second, then he said, 'But I don't like our president much right now. He embarrasses our great country.' I sensed we had stumbled on a sore spot, so I quickly changed the subject. Rod talked about first meeting American soldiers. 'We always worked so well with the Americans, and we were jealous of them! They got all of the girls, because they had all the money!' I laughed, and I asked Rod how much he was paid in the Army. I couldn't believe his answer. 'Six cents per day,' Rod said. I nearly choked on my drink when he said that. 'Six cents per day?' I asked him incredulously. He said it again, 'Yep, one half crown per week. Six cents per day, for putting our lives on the line.' Wow. I was blown away.

Rod has one daughter, Lynda, who recently retired in Michigan. She managed a beauty salon for many years. Rod is the remaining sibling. His younger brother Tony passed away on June 19, 2017.

Rod's hobbies today include golfing and swimming. Rod is more active than most people half his age. He swims nearly every day to maintain his strength. 'When you're over ninety, you have to work a little harder,' he said with a smile. As for his golf game, he said, 'Yeah, I enjoy playing, but I'm not very good. I used to be able to drive the ball a long way, but I can't hit it as far as I used to. These days, I usually shoot an 85 or an 87.' Again, I nearly choked on my drink. 'Not very good?' I asked. 'I would give any-thing to shoot an 85 or an 87.' 'He constantly has projects work-ing around the house,' Maureen said with a smile. 'He always has to stay busy.' Rod built an impressive workshop in his garage he uses for wood-working, mechanical projects, and do-it-yourself activities. Years ago, shortly after he returned from the war, Rod competitively raced motorcycles off-road in Great Britain. He owned a Norton motorcycle, and he raced on a team with three other guys.

At age twenty-three, he was racing at a nearby competition, and it was a tight race. He was travelling approximately 110 mph, and a little girl ran from the infield on to the track, right in front of Rod. He had to make an instant decision: either hit the little girl or lay the bike down. Guess which he chose? Rod said, 'I was doing great for about thirty feet, then it started to hurt. I felt this arm break, then that arm broke, then I felt my shoulders go. Then I remember laying there, and I was praying that none of the other bikes would hit me. They flew by all around and somehow they all missed me!' As a result of the accident, Rod broke nearly every bone in his body. He remained in a cast for nine months, with his arms sticking straight in the air. Rod's first wife, Jean, pregnant with their daughter Lynda, made Rod swear he would never again race motorcycles. Just one more amazing story.

Jean passed away in 1971 due to heart complications. In 1973, Rod married Maureen, and the two have been inseparable ever since.

We drifted back toward Rod's time in the war, and I asked Rod if he still carried any animosity toward the Germans. He replied, 'No, I have good friends who are German. The Germans have an in-herent superiority complex, but they are very good people.' Rod does, however, have great animosity for 'Field Marshall Mont-gomery,' the great British military leader who ultimately approved the plan for Operation Market Garden. 'I hated him,' Rod said in a serious tone. 'He was an egotistical maniac, and I didn't like him at all. Not just because of Operation Market Garden. In general, he had a big ego, and the soldiers ultimately suffered as a result. Montgomery and Patton hated each other, and they constantly battled for glory, which probably cost many Allied lives.

'I had the opportunity to meet General Omar Bradley [Commander of the U.S. First Army],' Rod said. 'He was a fantastic man. He was mild-manner, soft-spoken, but also very firm. I met him in Germany during the victory parade in Berlin. I learned a lot from General Bradley and his command-style. During my career, I tried to lead the same way: soft-spoken but also firm. General Bradley didn't have the ego of Patton or Montgomery, but he was an even more effective leader, in my opinion.' Bradley was nicknamed 'the G.I. General' by war correspondent Ernie Pyle, as he was known for his soften-spoken, unassuming manner. Eisenhower referred to Bradley as a 'master tactician,' and he entrusted Bradley with command of more troops than any general in American military history. Bradley had four armies, twelve corps, and forty-eight divisions under his command. A total of more than 1.3 million troops. He commanded the U.S. First Army Group from D-Day through V-Day in May 1945. It's remarkable that Rod had the opportunity to meet this incredible leader.

I asked Rod if he ever returned to Arnhem after the war. He replied, 'I've never been back to Arnhem. I've never really wanted to go back.' Rod continued, 'I've never really understood why the Germans destroyed the city of Arnhem.' In Rod's words, '10,000 soldiers went in from our division, and only 1,700 of us made it out.'

Rod smiled and said, 'many years after the war, I continued to think about Don Spall, killed right after we landed in Arnhem. I carried substantial guilt. I believed he was killed trying to help me. He was my best friend. We were living in Michigan at the time, and I was working for GM [This was approximately 40 years after the war]. I talked about Don often, and I asked Maureen one day, 'I wonder what Don would have looked like today?' Maureen decided to search for his records through her genealogy/ancestry hobby. Eventually, she found out that Don had survived, married a German lady, and resided in England for many years. Maureen attempted to contact Don's family and received a reply many years later. Don passed away just a few years before. Rod learned that Don survived his injuries and had been captured by the German's. He was held in a German POW camp for many years. The Germans saved his life by giving Don medical treatment. Rod talked about how lucky Don was to survive life in a German POW camp. Rod explained that the Germans usually treated the officers pretty well, but non-commissioned officers were typically treated badly.

Rod, one of the most positive people I've ever met, pauses again to reflect. He pointed to his belly button and discussed the wound that had been with him since that ill-fated mission in 1944. 'I have two belly buttons,' he said again with a jovial expression on his face. 'I used to joke with my buddies. Back in the day, when I was in good shape, I'd go swimming, and I'd take bets with people to see if they could figure out which of my belly buttons was the real one.' Rod won't stop laughing at this point. Next, he told me he plans to live to age 114, and at that point he said, 'I'm going to renegotiate the whole DAMN thing. Knowing what I know now, of course,' he continued to laugh. Rod decided to quit drinking many years ago, and now, instead of cold beer, he enjoys O'Doul's, a non-alcoholic beer. 'It tastes just like beer,' he told me. I'll have to try O'Doul's again sometime. I don't think I've had 'near-beer' (as we called it) since my Army days, deployed in Iraq. Alcohol wasn't allowed there, so 'near-beer' was the closest thing we were allowed to drink.

Rod doesn't believe in using guns for sport. Despite being a sharp-shooter, Rod hasn't fired a gun since the war, and he doesn't plan to. He grew serious for a second, and he looked me dead in the eye, 'I killed a lot of people,' he said. I responded, 'You had to. You had no choice.' Rod, then added, 'Well, I had to if we wanted to survive. I had the ultimate weapon. I was lucky to be chosen to carry the Bren gun. The Bren never jammed, and the range was clean and accurate up to 500 or 600 yards. The .303 round could penetrate through 12 inches of oak, yet the gun had very little recoil. Amazing.' Rod clearly loved the Bren, as he kept coming back to it over and over throughout our conversation, giving the Bren ample credit for his survival. 'The Bren saved my butt over and over again, many times,' he said again. Jumping back to today, Rod is deeply disturbed by the mass shootings taking place in our country. He can't understand why they happen or how they happen. After the war, Rod made a conscious effort to be a peaceful and non-violent person. I could sense that when I first met him. Rod fears the hate that is building in the U.S. today. It reminds him very much of what happened in Europe in the 1930's. He said, 'You have divided groups who are increasingly turning to violence to solve their problems. It's not a good situation, and it reminds me of what happened before World War II. I study history. I love history, and unfortunately, history tends to repeat itself.'

We exchanged other stories about weapons and equipment. I updated Rod on some of the technology our military uses today, such as thermal and night vision equipment. Many of Rod's important missions were at night, but instead of night vision, Allied artillery units would drop flares to light their path. We also had some good laughs telling stories about jumping out of planes. Both of us jumped only five times in our military careers. I jumped five times in training at Airborne School [Fort Benning, GA], and Rod jumped five times: four in training and one, well....his final jump wasn't in training. Rod remembers the first time he jumped in training, 'I landed so damn hard, I thought I broke both legs,' he told me. 'I remember the exact same feeling,' I laughed in response.

Rod said the British soldiers always wanted what the American soldiers had. 'We had two uniforms. One was for nicer occasions, and the other was for battle. Our battle uniform was a heavy-duty khaki material,' Rod explained. 'When we met the Americans, we saw they had a boot with a built-in Gator. Soon, every British soldier I knew was wearing the American boots. They were much better!' Rod described American soldiers as 'Great guys.' He mentioned they weren't as concerned with their appearance as British soldiers. 'American soldiers didn't usually worry about shaving and things like that. Their uniforms usually looked pretty bad. We were ordered to shave and maintain our uniforms. We were jealous of the Americans.' The same high standards applied to their daily practices in war. 'We were told to treat German prisoners with respect, and we were ordered to be humane. If someone was suffering, whether friend or foe, we were told to ensure they no longer had to suffer.'

Rod laughed about the English tradition of tea. 'The soldiers would stop in the middle of battle to have their afternoon tea,' Rod recalled in amazement. 'Believe it or not, I'm actually allergic to tea. When I was kid, my mother gave me tea. My skin had an allergic reaction, so one time, my mom rushed me to the doctor. The doctor asked me what I had to eat and drink that day, and finally, we figured out it was the tea. My younger brother had the exact same allergy. We are the only Englishmen I've ever heard of that are allergic to tea. Who knows, maybe it saved my life over there?'

Having never fired a gun after the war, Maureen and Rod went to a carnival one evening to relax and enjoy the atmosphere. They walked past the carnival games, and Maureen asked Rod if he could win a teddy bear for her. It was a shooting game, and Rod politely declined, saying that he hadn't touched a gun since the war. Maureen's persistence eventually convinced Rod to play the game. Rod said, 'It was a machine gun type-of-thing. There were fifty rounds, and usually people would squeeze the trigger once and all of the bullets would be gone. When I started, I fired one shot, and it was low and to the right. So, I made a compensation and adjusted upward and left. The center bullseye was red, and about this big [Rod demonstrated with his hands]. I adjusted my aim and ended up shooting the entire bullseye out of the target. I won the teddy bear, and the guy told me to never come back and shoot again!' Rod laughed. Then he grew serious. 'But, Maureen told me that my entire demeanor changed. Just like that. She said that I scared her. Like she didn't know who I was.' Maureen privately mentioned this same incident to me later as well. It clearly impacted both of them. It reinforced the immense strain those nine days in hell had inflicted on Rod.

In Rod's generation, PTSD [post-traumatic stress disorder] didn't exist. Some called it 'Shell Shock,' or 'Battle Fatigue,' but there was no official treatment program in place. Rod fought in Arnhem for nine days, and those nine days have haunted him for the rest of his life. 'I had nightmares for a long time,' Rod explained. 'I still have them. One time, I was yelling in the middle of the night and Maureen woke me up. She shook me, and when I awakened, I grabbed her by the throat. I had no idea where I was or what was happening. She wondered what the hell just happened. I apologized of course, and thankfully those things didn't happen often, but occasionally they rear their ugly head. I have had my problems, and I still do, but that's life.'

Maureen added to the story, 'I have a hint for other military spouses. To this day, when I wake Rod up, I only wake him up by shaking his feet.'

Rod also mentioned a coincidence that occurred sometime in the late 1960's, while Rod was at work. 'We were standing in line, and a guy behind me kept complaining about the inconveniences of being in the Army. I didn't say anything at first, but the man kept talking. Finally, I could feel the anger building inside me, so I turned to the man and said, 'You don't know what true fighting is all about. Have you ever heard of a place called Arnhem? That was true fighting.' The man immediately shut his mouth. Suddenly, a man further back in line asked, 'Hey, you were in Arnhem?' Then he said 'I was in Nijmegen.' I shook the man's hand, left the line, and we both proceeded to the nearest bar. We talked for the next twelve hours, and it was a breakthrough for both of us. I couldn't believe the coincidence.'

Maureen described this story as a 'no one understands' mentality. While Rod rarely discussed his Arnhem experiences with her, he met this man in line, and they spent the next twelve hours telling their most intimate combat stories. She believes this mentality is very common in soldiers from all generations. I happen to agree with her.

Herman, my friend and Rod's neighbor, told his story of meeting Rod for the first time. In 1995, Herman purchased the house next door, and when he was working in the garden one day, Herman heard a thunderous noise, turned around, and saw Rod flying into the yard on a huge motorcycle. With a big smile on his face, he shook Herman's hand, and they have been close friends and neighbors ever since. Other neighbors tell the story of the ninety-something year-old man climbing on top of his RV to replace the roof.

This is man who truly understands planes, trains and automobiles. Over the years he engineered and manufactured ships, automobiles, airplanes, trains, fighter jets, motorcycles, and to top it all off, a flying saucer!

Rod paused for a second. I could see his brain still reliving many of these stories. 'World War II was tough,' Rod said almost casually. 'Really tough. But, what you did was tough too. You guys go to war, come home, then go right back again. You do it over and over again. With us, it was simple. We were in a world war. We went off to war. We either died or survived, then we came home for good once the war was over. To go there, come home, then go back again, I think is cruel and wrong,' he said with a concerned expression on his face. I was embarrassed and appalled to think that Rod would consider anything we did in Iraq/Afghanistan as being 'tough'. What Rod and his fellow soldiers experienced was the epitome of the word 'tough'. I suppose there were some similarities, as both wars were very violent for their own reasons, but in today's war, the insurgents are trained to operate as ghosts, frequently attacking and then disappearing by blending into the civilian population. In Rod's war, they were fighting an equal, or superior, military force, lined up chest-to-chest, mano y mano. Now, our Army is very powerful, and we will most-likely win in the end, but in Rod's day, victory was not a foregone conclusion. Millions of men sacrificed their lives to achieve victory. They died to ultimately free the world from the black cloud of evil consuming it.

Throughout our conversation, I thanked Rod many times for his service. He countered by thanking me for my service, and he said, 'Thank you for keeping me safe.' I thanked him for keeping US safe, and I told him that none of us would exist today without his (and others) incredible heroism. I wished Rod 'Happy Veteran's Day', as it was Veteran's Day weekend. He told me he wasn't in the American Army, so he doesn't feel right standing up when people ask who served. I hold him that he needs to stand EVERY SINGLE TIME. He is a true hero who stood shoulder-to-shoulder with American heroes to rid the world of evil. Rod sacrificed so much in the name of freedom. In the future, he must stand proudly to receive the recognition he deserves. That was a direct order from an officer in the U.S. Army.

Thank you, Rod, for sacrificing so much. You have provided us with the greatest privilege on earth: **freedom**.

EPILOGUE

Beyond Arnhem

As we approach the 75th Anniversary of Operation Market Garden, Rod's story reminds us of the sacrifices made by those men on the ground. The men who gave so much to forge a direct path into the Third Reich. Rod and his brothers suffered through nine days of hell. They fought against all odds, and only a few made it out of Arnhem. Despite a nearly impossible mission, how did these men fight so valiantly? They were completely surrounded by Germans with no possible chance for victory, so why didn't they just surrender? What internal forces drove the men to continue fighting? What drove the men to fight at all? By this point in the war, they were fighting on German's turf, not their own. Surrender would have been easily justifiable, with no possible way for Rod's men to win. Yet, they continued to fight.

As I sat with Rod and listened to his story, these questions kept pinging in my head. I sit with other Veterans, and the same questions arise. Many of these men volunteered to join the military. They were on foreign soil [across the Atlantic Ocean for the Americans], and the sense of desperation should not have existed in the same sense as the Germans, who were protecting their homeland. Hitler was not initially threatened by the Allies, particularly the Americans, for these same reasons. He believed that without a true sense of desperation, there was no way to develop an effective combat soldier. Hitler's propaganda fueled the Wehrmacht, he believed, through love for their 'motherland.' At first, Hitler preached of spreading the motherland's power and resources, through a unification of Europe under one mighty German government. Then, as the Allies began to surround Germany, his message quickly changed to 'protecting the motherland from the evil invaders who wish to corrupt mighty Germany.' Through his spread of propaganda, Hitler believed German forces would be unstoppable. In the end, they were not. Germany possessed a very strong military. One of the strongest the world had ever seen, but the might of their military eventually succumbed to the strength of the Allies.

The mighty German war machine focused on developing rigid, disciplined soldiers. Robots trained to follow orders and execute tasks, without fail. They were expected to react without thinking and hold ground at all costs. Yet, in the end, their defenses collapsed. They surrendered in droves. How did this happen, while under opposite circumstances, Rod and his men fought for days without food, water, and ammunition? The answer lies in Rod's story. During Rod's toughest days, who does he mention? George Joy, his close friend and battle buddy. They lived, fought, and bled together. More than 40 years later, Rod wondered what happened to his friend Don Spall. Why did Don suddenly pop into Rod's head? Because Rod and his men fought for a greater purpose. They fought for one another. They cared for one another. The guilt Rod carried stayed with him for all of those years. When darkness descended upon the Allies, they had nowhere else to turn.

When I meet these great Veterans, they are clearly proud to have served their country. When I ask them who they were fighting for, or what drove them, they don't usually discuss national pride, ridding the world of evil, and other grand, romantic notions. In the midst of combat, they talk about their friends, battle buddies, and the men to their right and left. These deep-rooted relationships fueled our men to push forward, to continue fighting, and to never give up. These feelings are different than our traditional, romantic understanding of 'love.' In many ways, these feelings are stronger. They are impossible to describe, unless one has actually been in combat. If so, they are easily understood.

I would like to briefly discuss the condition we now call PTSD (Post Traumatic Stress Disorder). While Rod's military career spanned longer than nine days, nine days of hell in Arnhem scarred Rod for the remainder of his life. They caused him to become a different man. Rod lives what appears to be a perfect life. He is an incredibly cheerful and positive man. He is a great husband, a great father, and he has accomplished more than most could ever dream. Yet, somewhere hidden deep inside, Rod struggles to suppress memories, feelings, and actions from just nine days, seventy-five years ago. Rod has been on this earth for more than 33,500 days at the time of writing, and yet, these few days continue to haunt him. Rod still deals with nightmares today, and like lightning, his mind sometimes transports Rod back to Arnhem. He shot a toy gun to win Maureen a stuffed animal at the carnival, which was the first gun Rod fired since the war. Immediately, he was transported back to Arnhem. Those nine days were so brutal for Rod, they clearly made a permanent impression on his mind. While not a recognized condition at the time, Rod described PTSD in its' truest form.

When I meet Veterans like Rod, I observe these two issues working hand-in-hand. Our brains naturally develop senses of attachment to certain people, and under incredibly difficult, life-threatening circumstances, the bonds grow even stronger. Therefore, when a loss occurs, the pain magnifies itself many times over. I've heard Veterans [from all wars] express these same feelings over-and-over. It's not death and violence that seems to keep their minds from moving forward. The strength of the bonds formed with other human beings, combined with the impact of death and violence on those bonds, prevents their minds from moving forward.

When I deployed into combat, we frequently experienced death and violence. We witnessed people dying in front of us, even women and children. Sometimes on a daily basis. While those moments weren't pretty and occasionally pop into my head, what moments keep me awake at night? What moments drill to the center of my core? The loss of my men. My fellow soldiers, young kids, who had their lives taken from them abruptly, for no good reason. Based on Rod's story, my own experiences, and the stories of other Veterans like Rod, I have drawn the conclusion that these feelings are the culprit. These feelings prevent Veterans from truly moving forward.

To this day, my unit has lost more soldiers from suicide than combat, and we continue to lose men each year. Many of Rod's fellow soldiers returned home, never to be heard-from again. If nine days of hell can affect Rod in such a profound way, think of the millions of other soldiers who experienced similar situations throughout the past century. Try to quantify the sheer volume of pain and suffering caused as a result of these wars. What permanent mark has been left on these men and society? Answer: Twenty-two. The number, twenty-two.

Twenty-two Veterans take their lives each day in the United States. Twenty-two of the greatest men and women our society has produced. Twenty-two men and women remove their beautiful souls from this earth. After surviving vicious battles with the Germans, Japanese, North Koreans, Vietnamese, terrorists and other deadly enemies, their lives are taken by a silent killer. A killer in the form of an unshakeable remnant from the past.

Rod was a lucky one. He was able to keep the darkness suppressed inside. He has lived an incredibly happy and productive life. Many Veterans are not able to do so. They fight an internal battle, every day, until the darkness eventually overtakes them.

As I continue my journey to meet our nation's greatest heroes, I want to hear their incredible military stories. Sharing these stories is a passion and priority for me. An even greater passion, however, is to examine the internal challenges these men face. The challenges they overcame to blend back into society, to live somewhat normal lives. Now these men live among us in quiet neighborhoods, nursing homes, and even our own neighborhoods. We see them each day in grocery stores, restaurants, and nearly everywhere we go. These men carry massive weights on their shoulders, and to move forward as a society, we owe them at least a minimal recognition of this burden. We may never fully understand it, but we need to acknowledge it.

One way to acknowledge this burden is to say two simple words. 'Thank you.' By simply saying 'thank you,' we can provide instant acknowledgment of the sacrifice they have made for us. Many of these brave men have outlived their families. They are in their nineties and have outlived their children in many cases. When carrying such a burden, the worst possible feeling is solitude, the feeling of being alone. A simple 'thank you' can immediately erase any feeling of loneliness. Why? It chips away at the hidden burden they are carrying. It provides a brief ray of light into the darkness lying deep inside their souls. Most of all, it provides unspoken affirmation that the pain they carry is worth it. Remember Rod's 'no one understands' mentality? By simply saying 'thank you,' you may not fully understand, but you will achieve a bond with these men that conveys understanding. Two short words can keep the darkness at bay. They will feel it in their hearts.

Only then, have we done our part. Only then, can we truly walk among heroes.

Thank you, Rod.

Rod (left) and his George Joy taken during the Victory Day Parade in Berlin.

Rod and author, Jeff Wells.

Rod next to the Commando Monument that sits on
their training ground in Scotland.

Works Cited

Beevor, Antony. *The Battle of Arnhem, The Deadliest Airborne Operation of World War II.* New York, NY. Penguin Publishing Group, 11 September 2018. Print.

Campagna, Palmiro. *The Avro Arrow, For the Record.* Toronto, Ontario, Canada. Dundurn, 2019. Print.

Dunning, James. *The British Commandos, The Origins and Special Training of an Elite Unit.* Paladin Press, July 1, 2007. Print.

Middlebrook, Martin. *Arnhem 1944: The Airborne Battle, 17-26 September.* New York, NY. Penguin Books Ltd, September 28, 1975. Print.

Made in the USA
Middletown, DE
29 September 2019